Figure 1 Dorothy Margaret Nicholas - Age 19

For my family

Copyright © 2023
©Diana Helen Pritchard
Published by ShortCliff
https://shortcliffpoetry.com

ISBN: 978-1-9196144-5-8

Figure 2 Sample of Envelopes

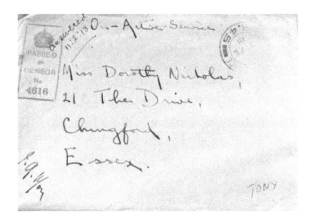

Figure 3 Passed by the Censor

In Memory of Dorothy Margaret Nicholas

1896 to 1946

A Discovery

A black faux-leather writing case,
dusky orange Defence-of-the-Realm
permit book tucked firmly
behind ink-stained blotting paper.

Miss Dorothy Margaret Nicholas.
Five feet four inches.
Female, Slim, Hair- dark brown.
Eyes - brown, no distinctive marks.
Photograph of a young woman
in a Red Cross Nurse Uniform.

And now I remove the letters
from small, buff envelopes
addressed - Brookfield Red X Hospital
marked - ARMY POST OFFICE
stamped –PASSED by CENSOR

Dozens of them,
and on each, my grandmother's
diligently dated note - 'ANSWERED'

© Diana Helen Pritchard 2012

Figure 4 Map of The Western Front WW1

TABLE OF CONTENTS

INTRODUCTION

DOROTHY MARGARET NICHOLAS

My grandmother, Dorothy, was a Red Cross Nurse in WW1 and corresponded with a number of servicemen who had been recovering at the hospital where she worked. She kept the letters in a black faux leather case along with two albums of photos. The letters were passed to me and I set to copying and transcribing them. I found them to be quite fascinating, giving an insight into how the men were encouraged to go to war, some of them volunteering or enlisting when underage. They seemed to encourage each other to get better so they could return to join their friends, as I could see from the letters that several of them knew each other. Their letters were often sent from the Western Front, some from the Trenches where they had returned after convalescing or from other convalescent homes, still waiting to go back to the war. From being rather young and naïve in their early letters some appeared to be quite disillusioned by the end of the war. One of them, Tony, was a family friend who was later to marry Dorothy's cousin Alison Duff Duncan, and another, Fred, was a cousin. Letters written by Fred to his friend Ben were also sent to me by Anne Lee which I have included.

Each letter has been given a title based on its content and arranged in chronological order. I have also made a few notes about each serviceman. The letters are in sets for each individual.

At the back of the book, I have included a biography about Dorothy and how she came to be a Red Cross Nurse. Also, I have made a brief note about her parents and family.

I have endeavoured to keep true to their letters without interpreting them in any way so that the reader can make their own mind up about the feelings and struggles, the happy times and the losses experienced by the men through their written words. As far as I am aware, none of them were poets. I have, however, created a short poem of my own using one of Tony's letters and using some of his words.

Most of the photos are from Dorothy's own photo album and some were sent to me by my brother, William Filip Moen, who holds a quantity of family memorabilia.

There are several references to Moll or Mollie who was Dorothy's younger sister and was 6 years old at the start of the war.

The Hale End Red Cross Hospital

Also referred to as *Brookfield*

1914-1919

The Hale End Red Cross Hospital for convalescent servicemen opened in 1915 in the grounds of Brookfield House, Oak Hill, Woodford, Essex. The owner of the house, Mr. Thomas Sutcliffe Armstrong, had donated the land, as well as contributing to the cost of the building, in memory of his son who had been killed in the war. Mrs. Henry Young of Larkshill Farm, Chingford, gave £100 for the linen, and further funds for the upkeep of the Hospital were given by Mr. Charles Merriam of the Xylonite Company (xylonite is better known by its American name as celluloid).

The Hospital, which also became known as the Brookfield Red Cross Hospital, had 30 beds. It was equipped and maintained by the Hale End District Association, which had been founded as a ratepayers' association in 1909. The Hospital was administered by a management committee according to the rules of the Red Cross Society.

The Hospital closed in February 1919

Hale End is a locality in East London in the borough of Waltham Forest, very near Woodford Green, two miles from Tottenham and one mile from Walthamstow. It adjoins Highams Park in the E4 postal district. Much of Highams Park until the late 19th century used to be called Hale End. (Wikipedia)

Figure 5 Brookfield - From Dorothy's Photo Album

Figure 6 Dorothy Outside Brookfield Hospital

After the Billiard Match

*Brooks, Booth, **Nickie**, Bell, Harris,
Bartle, Bentley, Buckle, Bowness & Martin*

Figure 7 Crutch Cases 1918

*Betts – see letter

Letter from France

15th December 1917
Passed by the Censor
On active service

Dear Dorothy,

> *student songs*
> *to psalm tunes*

horses standing out in the open,
at least the tops of them are

> *the feet and legs*
> *being well out of sight*
> *in the mud.*

I'm in the muddiest country
> *in the world*
but   after all

"c'est la guerre."

.   ...Tony

© By Diana Pritchard

TONY

Lieutenant JAMES ANTONY MORE

Figure 8 Lieutenant James Antony More

Tony was born on the 3rd May 1894 to James Elder More (Grocer and Wine Merchant) and Margaret Montgomery More Nee McLeod. Living at 7 St. Mary Street, St. Andrews, Fife. After the war he became a university lecturer and he died 23rd May 1947 Dalkeith, Midlothian. His son's name, Brian M. More was registered on Death Certificate. He married Alison Young Duncan on 23 September 1924 whose father was Robert Fleming Duncan and mother was Ellen Duff Duncan. Robert's mother was called **Alison** Robertson. At time of their marriage, they were living at The Dene, Park Road, Eskbank, Dalkeith. He Retired from service on the 5th December 1923. Tony became a University Lecturer and lectured in Canada in 1923 when he was 29 years old.

Received the Officers' Victory Medal for France 20.03.18. Was a Lieutenant – Also the British Medal – sent to address 10 George Square, Edinburgh.

Royal Garrison Artillery during World War 1

The Royal Garrison Artillery

At the end of the 19th century the Royal Garrison Artillery, which was part of the Royal Artillery, was divided into 3 Divisions:

The Eastern Division, HQ at Dover. Depot companies at Dover and Great Yarmouth.
The Southern Division, HQ at Portsmouth. Depot companies at Gosport and Seaforth (near Liverpool).
The Western Division, HQ at Devonport. Depot companies at Plymouth and Scarborough.

The Garrison Artillery was composed of 104 service companies in 1900, forty of them in the UK, 37 in various colonies of the Empire and 27 in India. A company was commanded by a major with 6 or so officers, around 10 NCOs and 100 to 200 men.

The uniform of Garrison Artillery was the same as Field Artillery except that they were more likely to wear trousers instead of boots and breeches. On their shoulder straps were the initials of the name of their division and the number of their company.

The RGA developed from fortress-based artillery located on British coasts. From 1914 when the army possessed very little heavy artillery it grew into a very large component of the British forces. It was armed with heavy, large calibre guns and howitzers that were positioned some way behind the front line and had immense destructive power.

The Heavy Batteries of the RGA
The Siege Batteries of the RGA
The Mountain Batteries of the RGA
The Anti-Aircraft Artillery of the RGA
The Royal Marine Artillery
RGA Companies at home and in Empire

Sheringham Training

22nd November 1916 *Answered*
7.12.16

Officers' Mess, 2 1st Highland (Fife)R.G.A.
 (Royal Garrison Artillery)
Sheringham, Norfolk

Dear Dorothy,

How long is it since I saw you in St. A. and promised to write and let you know that the war was still leaving me alive and kicking.

Sometimes I hear from Moll that she has been to a picture show, or that someone near St. Andrews is dead, or that Mrs. Fowler has produced a baby. Moll is a cure and no mistake!

This place, Sheringham is Top hole in Summer but now that the cold weather has set in it is pretty awful. Our winter quarters are a mile and a half from Sheringham. We occupy a group of farms which are more or less close together – we had to go to an out of the way spot to find stables for the horses.

Having vegetated for several months now I feel like a burst in town. It would be jolly I could meet you one weekend and go to some show or another. I don't know anyone in London and mooning round on one's own isn't a bit of a pleasure. Would your people let you off on the loose?

Has Jack Duncan ever been to see you since he and Duncan got lost in London? I haven't seen Jack since I met him in Norwich in June.

As far as I can make out our battery is to be left at home as a training unit, which means that men will constantly be passing through our hands and we, who do the training, will remain in Norfolk until the end of the Great War.

All the supervisory officers from this battery are already off to new regular batteries which are being pushed out to France every week. UGH! I'm fed up

Cherry O, Dorothy

Yours sincerely

Tony   PS. They've given me a second "pipe" which will enable me to luxuriate in Gold Flake instead of Woodbines.

New Orders for Officers

14th December 1916

Officers' Mess, 2 1st Highland (Fife)R.G.A.
(Royal Garrison Artillery)
Sheringham, Norfolk

Answered
14.02.1917

Dear Dorothy,

The Major has asked me to take my seven days leave just now instead of sometime in the New Year. My intention was to have a London weekend before Christmas and have a good time after being shut up in this quiet little corner for so many months.

So, Dorothy, my weekend is off at present. Thank your mother for me for her kind offer of hospitality. I would have been delighted to have accepted it. Sometimes, I hope, I may.

Have you seen any of the new orders for Officers on leave in London? I doubt they wash out all the chances of a very great "burst"! No dinner to cost more than 5/6, no dancing and no mufti – the war **is** coming home to us at last.

Things in the Battery are quiet. Ashton, our serving Sub, has lost his best girl – she has become engaged to a fellow with red tabs at the War Office. Result – our Ashton has turned into a bear and has gone off his food. Have your feelings ever made you like that, Dorothy? I'm sorry I'm so inexperienced. The Major is in a good mood and has presented the men with turkeys for Christmas. The Captain has gone off to S. Wales on leave and he swore, before he left, that he wouldn't be sober until he slept it off in the train coming back – the Capt. Is an awful "bird" bit is *un bon soldat*."

Fancy Duncan being in France? You remember how Jack and I used to think we were old soldiers when Dunc was looking after sheep – and Magpie Arms.

Cheery O Dorothy,

I wish you a very merry Christmas and no colic.

Yours, Tony

Empire's Might

29th November 1917 Tony

9th Heavy Battery R.G.A. B.E.F.
(Royal Garrison Artillery) British Expeditionary Forces.
On Active Service

Censor No. 4616

21 The Drive, Chingford, Essex.

Dear Dorothy,

This evening I had nothing on earth to do so I commenced to rummage about amount some old papers, bootlaces and cough drops which had accumulated in my kit bag during the past two years. I came upon a letter and turning it over, I noticed "Dorothy." I won't say how many loving things preceded "Dorothy" or how many crosses and things succeeded your fair signature. My ardour (*sic*) being kindled, I determined to write to you. If you give me my desert, you'll never answer this but I pray that you'll forgive me and tell me how the world is using you. Do you wonder what you have to forgive? Your letter is dated 12.2.17 and it is my turn to write. Comprenez?

Well you will see from my address that the Army Council was not satisfied with the progress of the war and determined to put the Empire's might into the field. In other words I got a telegram to quit Blighty.

Since coming out here I've had a glorious time wangling late passes at the Base and dining with the boys; sometimes endeavouring to say nice things in French to pretty girls; living on hard tuck and water for days and sitting to a flank watching the horrible Hun blowing up my happy home. Well, c'est la guerre! Which, translated, means "things might be wary" The *gh* in might being pronounced like the r in tomato. I feel facetious!

At present I'm in a delightful billet with an earthen floor and the odour of cows. The place is quite Irish in the way a few stray hens share my abode; but it is not so clean as most Irish abodes – sounds bad? In spite of the billet and a few other minor worries I am going strong and waxing rich in experience.

What about the WAAC Dorothy? Am I going to see you somewhere behind the line looking after stray subs and occasional Brass Hats? There are heaps of English girls at the bases but we are not allowed to speak to them.   I think, however, we could manage it surreptitiously if we were given a chance.

With kindest regards to "Nick" and your mother.

Yours sincerely,

Tony

 PS My address is: 9th Heavy Battery, R.G.A, B.E.7

Love and War

15.12.17 Tony

On Active Service
Censor No. 4616   *Answered 29.12.17*

Addressed to 21 The Drive, Chingford, Essex.

Dear Dorothy,

I received your letter which came safe and sound with great rejoicings: you see I thought, from my previous behaviour that I might get a reply in the spring.

I'm extremely happy at present as I've fallen very much in love with une jeune fille Francais. Since writing you last the battery has been rather unsettled and at present I'm living in luxury in the farm of the young lady's father. As I've forgotten most of the French I ever knew I find it rather difficult to say the nice things that I'd be able to say to you but we get on wonderfully with our bad French and our gesticulations. Of course, there is no use eulogizing the girl to you as I question if girls understand each other. I'll have to write to Jack and he'll be able to understand. By the way we have dances and songs and all sorts of merrymakings. I sing student's drinking songs to psalm tunes and they think I'm a very devout young feller – what a life!

You must give my love to your friend who works on the railway. I rather expect he'll be called up before the war is over so you'll have him to write to him too.

Our horses are standing out in the open, at least the tops of them are, the feet and legs being well out of sight in mud. I'm in the muddiest country in the world! But, after all "c'est la guerre."

I'm glad MBD is having a good time in Edin. I must write her and tell her how lovely I am and see if I can get her to send her "kindest regards." I don't know Megs address or I might send her a stick of rock for Christmas.

By the way, you won't hear from me until after Christmas now so I wish you and Nick and your mother all the seasons good wishes.

Cheerio, Tony

Polished Buttons and Tight Boots

9th January 1918

No Envelope

Dear Dorothy,

My charming love affair is all over and I am now a broken-hearted wretch. Cruel fate has separated me from the fair one and I do nothing but pine and cherish fond memories. Bow wow! As a matter of fact there is only a temporary interruption. You see Madam, her mother, asked me to come for a couple of days whenever I could get off and at present I'm behaving myself awfully well so that the C.O. will repay me with a weekend holiday. Then I'll polish up my buttons and put on my tight boots and high me to my beloved.

I had one day off about a week ago when I jumped on a motor lorry and succeeded in getting about twenty miles behind the line and back to congratulations. Then I ate such a big lunch that I had to go to a picture show to sleep it off, and just at the entrance to the show I ran into the arms of an old chum called Bogach? It is grand to meet a friendly face out here- we had high old times together. He, like myself, was just out of the line for one day's joy.

I admire you girls who are doing war work such as nursing awfully much. I'm glad you like it too, Dorothy.

I hear that Meg Duncan is shortly leaving **Bangour*** for good and that she wants to go out to France. Jack seems to have been up there on leave for a few days. He went to see mother and told her that he was going to write shortly – he always is going to write. I suppose you get the same treatment from him.

 I am truly thankful that someone has a "Gerald" to encourage you to write occasionally. I think I must find out more about him and send him a box of cigars or some …..drops.

Do you like jam drops. I do most dreadfully – I'm always afraid, thou' that people think I'm eating them as a deodorant after I've had a wee droppie.   People are really horribly suspicious.!

I think you'd be doing an awful good turn of asking your friend the railway man to give me the addresses of his two daughters so that I can start a lively correspondence and perhaps induce them to court another soldier in "Ferhance"(*sic*).

Kindest regards to your mother, Nick and the engine driver.

Chin Chin!

Tony

Author's note: Meg Duncan was a nurse at Bangour Mental Hospital. Jack, referred to in this letter, was Dorothy's brother.

Bangour Mental Hospital

Bangour Mental Hospital (Bangour War Hospital) became one of the most important and renowned military hospitals in the kingdom *(The British Journal of Nursing April 20, 1918, p 277)*

Formation

By the beginning of the twentieth century the problem of mental illness in Edinburgh had become acute, and the need for a new psychiatric hospital was pressing. Situated 14 miles from Edinburgh in hilly woodlands, Bangour, near Broxburn, was the ideal place for such a hospital. The hospital was to be modelled on the Alt-Scherbitz asylum near Leipzig in Germany, but the first buildings were constructed hurriedly and were very basic temporary structures. The first patients from the Royal Edinburgh Asylum were transferred to Bangour in 1904, and the hospital was officially opened on
3rd October 1906.

In 1915 Bangour Village Hospital was taken over by the War Office as a military hospital. Its patients were transferred to asylums around the country. The numbers of staff and beds were increased substantially to cater for the influx of wounded soldiers who began to arrive in June of that year. By 1918 the hospital had reached a record capacity of 3000 patients, crammed into wards, huts and specially erected marquees.
Among the military patients treated at the hospital was Ivor Gurney, the war poet.

Dr Harvey Cushing, an American doctor who has left an extensive record of his war service, founded a Brain Injuries Unit at Bangour.

18th February 1918

Dear Dorothy,

Placed on the table before me I have your last letter and immediately under my nose is the envelope. Now the stamp is stuck on at an extraordinary angle and not being well versed in the mysterious messages conveyed by stamps, I request that you tell me at the end of your next letter what it is all about. I am really a most inquisitive person and things I don't understand worry me dreadfully – poor me!

Mother sends me the St. Andrews "Citizen" weekly and I notice the names of Misses Ena and Nancy Duncan in a column of the names of fortunates who have gained prizes during the local talent? week. Bravo! for the **Balrymonth** family. I wish to goodness I had some money to put in a War Loan. I'm saving up to get my watch out of pawn just now and after that I try to get enough to buy a War Savings Certificate. I'll have to be careful then or I'll be charged income tax!

Did I tell you that I expect to get leave sometime next month? What a terrible time I mean to have! I think I'll go to the pictures in St .Andrews and I may even go to the cafe for tea. Gee, I'm some bad lad!

Are there any good shows in town just now? I don't expect to be in London but if I am you mustn't get the fright of your life if I appear in your doorway and threaten to take you up to London to a show. We are having a good time just now. You see I'm getting a turn at our wagon lines and they are a safe distance from the Boche.

Cheery O,

LUV Tony.

Author's note: The Duncans were cousins to Dorothy

Pipe and Tobacco Ration

23rd May 1918 Tony   *Answered*
11.2.18

On Active Service
Passed by Censor No 4641
Army Post Office

Dear Dorothy,

I know that it is very much my turn to write you. Your last letter seems to have got lost in the war – I usually keep letters until I answer them – so if you asked me any questions be sure to ask them again next time.

I'm sorry for poor old Duncan. Being near to you must make a great difference to him. Give him my kindest regards and tell him I hope to see him at the harvest this year yet.

For the last ten days we've had scorching hot weather – the hottest I remember for years. You should see us strolling about at midday with no jackets or collars on and our shirts turned down showing glad necks. I'm as brown as a nut and absolutely fit.

About the middle of the hot spell we had a two-day train journey which made the poor old **horses** look pretty seedy. I rather think a third day in the train would have turned some of them.

The country here is hilly with fine rivers. We are camped just a little way from a river where we bathe every day. The current is too strong to swim up-stream but we kick along with the current until we feel tired and then crawl ashore and walk back to our clothes – it's great fun! We expect to be in action tomorrow but after our rest we feel fit for anything.

I had a letter from Mollie telling me that Jack has gone to India. I wish to goodness I had been able to go out East to see the country. I'm afraid after the war we'll be too hard up to travel as much as we'd like to.

The dreadful war this Spring has chased all my French sweethearts away to safer places. I was beginning to be able to flirt admirably in a broken language. Now I have only my pipe and my ration of tobacco to console me!

Did you ever read the book about the man who loved his life and adored a lady? The lady would have nothing to do with him unless he gave up his pipe. He determined to yield to her wishes but first of all decided to bid farewell to his pipe by sitting at home smoking it steadily for a fortnight.

After the fortnight he flung away – the lady.

Cheery O

Tony

Land of Landladies

31.01.18 Tony

Answered 11.2.18

(No Envelope)

Dear Dorothy,

I was dreadfully amused when you expressed a desire, in your last letter, to know if I had done any active service yet. I can't write about it of course but our battery has just pulled out to rest after five weeks as thin a time as anyone can wish for. Never mind, we're still merry and bright as possible on French small beer and ration cigarettes.

I'm back in the land of landladies and good luck to them. The daughter of the house is dreadfully bold and comes prancing into my bedroom at seven every morning armed with a cup of coffee and good wishes for the day. When first I suffered this performance, I, of course felt dreadfully nervous and hid under the sheets, but I soon found that that Mlle. Was not to be outdone and I had to sit up and take my beverage while the good lady sat on the table swinging her feet (tres chic too) about and encouraging my atrocious French.

I'm positive, you know Dorothy, that my defences will be carried one of those days and I'll have to hang up my hat in this land, far far from home.

Is there a chance of Meg Duncan coming out to France? It is three months since I last saw a W.A.A.C and I suppose that if any of you did manage to get out here I would have no chance of seeing you.

LUV

Tony

SWEETNAM

Private GEORGE LEONARD SWEETNAM

Private George Leonard Sweetnam. Reg No 23593, Royal
Warwickshire Regiment. Date of birth was 2 January 1898
Devonport, Plymouth. The following information on him is taken
from his obituary. He died on 4th March 1986. aged 88.

"He volunteered to join Kitchener's army shortly before the
introduction of conscription. He spent two periods in the front-line
trenches seeing action at Ypres and Passchendaele. He was
wounded in the battle but was maimed; his hearing was all but
destroyed; his left leg was peppered with fragments of shrapnel,
much of which remained in situ for the rest of his life. After a long
period of sick leave, he was sent back to the front. In 1918 at the
age of 20 he was de-mobbed. He was only **16 years old** when he
enlisted."

In my research in August 2012 I posted the following information to
the Great War Forum https://www.greatwarforum.org/topic/

*"I think I may be able to help narrow down the dates of some of
Sweetnam's postings during 1918. My grandmother was a nurse at
Brookfield Red Cross Hospital at Hale End. She received 9 letters from an L.
Sweetnam 23593, the first being from K. Coy, 36 Hut, 2nd R. Warwick R, 2
Camp Perham Downs, Nr. Andover, Kent. This letter is undated. The next
one was dated 03.02.18 from Singholm and the third from Dover Castle on
01.05.18. The next letter was from the Front and was censored as were the
all the rest.*

*He then seems have been with C. Coy, 16th R Warwicks BEF and the letter
dated 11th June 1918 stated that they left on 2nd June and was billeted to
a barn by the side of a canal. He also mentions that it was different to the
Front where he was in October 1917. Also that there was 'much spying
going on'. His last letter dated 1st November 1918 tells of there being very
few civilians in the place but that now that the Boshe have left they are
returning to their homes. He also doubts he will be 'back in civilian clothes
very soon'. My grandmother answered the letter on 18th November 1918*

but there are no further letters from him. Of course the letters reveal very little."

I hope this helps.   Diana Pritchard

23593 Pte. Sweetnam, George L. was awarded the Victory Medal and British War Medal.

The document states that he served in the 10th Bn.R. War.R, 2nd Bn.R. War.R and the 16th Bn.R.War.R. It further states that the medal was returned and scrapped on 13th May 1948.

He was also underage when he enlisted before conscription so this may have been the reason for not receiving the Silver Medal for those injured in the war.

*In **January 1916,** the Military Service Act was passed. This imposed conscription on all single men aged between 18 and 41, but exempted the medically unfit, clergymen, teachers and certain classes of industrial worker.*

Singholm Park Red Cross V.A.D. Hospital

41 Naze Park Road, Walton-on-the-Naze, Essex.   (Also known as the 'Home of Rest')

In 1904, Thomas Holmes formed the 'Home Workers' Aid Association' and took out a lease on the adjoining villa – to expand the original Home next door.   By 1909, work began on building a new Home.   A substantial part of the cost for this build was met by a Mr. Paris E Singer – who was a generous supporter of the aforementioned Association.

At the outbreak of the First World War, holidays at 'Singholme' (sic) were discontinued and the property became a Voluntary Aid Detachment convalescent home for soldiers under the control of the British Red Cross.   The British Red Cross Card for the hospital shows it administered to a maximum of 70 beds.

https://greatwarhomehospitals.wordpress.com

Fun in the Snow

January 1918

Singholm RC.H., Walton on Naze, Essex

Dear Nurse Nicholas,

Seeing I now have your address, kindly given me by Nurse Hawke, I am trying to write a few lines to you, although it is almost impossible, for the noise the fellows are making here is simply deafening. Thank you for that packet of toffee you put in my hand on leaving.   This place is nothing like Brookfield there aren't half as many nurses here, nor are they half as nice. Doesn't matter where you go, you won't find another staff nurse to come up to you at Brookfield. You are more than splendid. I hear you have been having snow & having some fun with it too. Well I only wish I'd been there; Nurse Hawke wouldn't have got the chance of putting one down my neck. We also have had a very heavy fall of snow, but there was no snowballing here. Personally I shall be glad when it all cleared away. Hope you haven't been taken ill with that meat you have been having at the hospital as I want a reply to this note. The noise is getting too loud so will close, hoping to hear from you soon.

Yours Sincerely,

      L Sweetnam.   (Answered 21:1:18)

Not Leaving Here Yet

8th February 1918
Singholm,

Dear Nurse,

Many thanks for your letter received on Friday. If I have to wait for another air raid before I receive another letter from Nurse Hawke, I hope we shall have one pretty soon, otherwise I may have to wait for ever. Hope Betts* is well on the road to recovery after his operations. What has Sister been telling you about my coming to see you all. You will be having a week off this week won't you after your fortnight spell of night duty. Shall not be leaving here for another week or so yet so expect you will be on duty. I guess you have had a fairly busy fortnight what with air raids and ...move into bed for breakfast, a little work won't do you any harm at any rate. No more news at present so will close, hoping to hear from you soon.

Yours sincerely,

L Sweetnam

Author's note – Betts and Sweetnam knew each other so they must have spent a period of time at Hale End together in order to have known Dorothy.*

Photo Swaps

Singholm R.C.H., Walton on Naze, Essex

Dear Nurse

Many thanks for letter of the 21st inst. I suppose if I hadn't written you first I should never have received a letter from you. Thank you for answering it so prompt, hope you'll do this same with this. Yes I remember him, he was a major. Sergt Howe was marked C.D. by him I believe also Harding. I've only heard so far that Harding, Hawkins & Harvey are marked C.D and Robinson C.H. Haven't heard any more about Collier so I suppose he can't be marked out, hope not at any rate. Everybody thinks the photos are good, sorry but haven't any left, or otherwise you should have one. How do you like the enclosed, had it taken by special request. It's purely a selfish motive that I've sent this to you, in return I want one of yours please. Now if you can't oblige, send it back please, I have one of Nurse Hawke, Nurse Armstrong, Sister Dowler is going to forward on hers, as soon as she gets them and also Nurse Anstey and I want yours as well please. Which do you think the best, this one, or the other which Nurse Hawke has. Haven't heard from Collier yet, you may tell him I'm expecting a letter by every post. Did they have to take the nurse from morning duty and put her on night as Nurse Hawke says they had to put another on on night, seeing I had left. I should think you were glad that that soldier whose name begins with S and ends with M had gone seeing you were so terrified of him. We have whist drives here every Saturday evening from 6 till about 8.30. Last night we had a concert party here (32n Fatigues) who were all soldiers stationed here. 3 hrs. good entertainment 6.30 till 9.30. Must now close as such long letters aren't always good for anyone (especially nurses).

Yours Sincerely L. Sweetnam.

PS Don't forget photo please.

Praise for Sister Dowler

23593 K Coy. 36 Hut, 2 R. Warwick R.,
2 Camp,
Perham Downs, Nr. Andover, Kent.

Saturday.

(No date) Assume 10th May 1918

Dear Nurse,

Very many thanks for your interesting letter which came on Friday morning. There are plenty of worse spots to be found in France if not in England and thank you for wishing me a log stay here for safety's sake. I couldn't help smiling to myself when you told Sister Hawke you were going to write and tell me you had never been on duty with such a cross sister just before that you said I was right in saying you had a very good time on night duty, otherwise you wouldn't have stayed on so long. All the same I know you are very sorry to lose her, I should have been too if I had been at Brookfield still, though I sincerely hope the next will be alright, but you couldn't wish for a better Sister than *Sister Dowler*. You nurses never had a job of waking that patient called Sweetnam, it was the Sister who only had the privilege of doing that and bringing him a nice hot cup of tea, (what are you smiling for) Very pleased to hear of Riseborough being marked C.W. a good route march with full pack may do him good but I don't think he will see much of that again. Wrote Nurse Hawke a few days ago, had I thought I should have received a letter from her without writing again. I think I should have waited for it and then written perhaps I shall receive two in return or else an extra-long one. Hope you put a jerk into it and wrote your five letters - thank you for writing mine first. Hope you haven't forgotten that promise when you have your photo taken. Today has been the warmest we have had for a few weeks, couldn't enjoy it much, as I am on dining room duty, tomorrow will be my half day. Anybody would think I was a nurse in hospital, talking about dining room duty. Wonder who's on duty at Brookfield now. Must now draw to a close, hoping to hear from you soon. Yrs. Sincerely, L. Sweetnam.

Waiting at Dover Castle

1st May 1918

C Coy 26 Hut, 4th R. Warwicks,
North Fall Meadow Camp,
Dover, Kent.

Dear Nurse,

Many thanks for letter, received two days ago. It had been delayed a little, as it had been readdressed home and then here. Evidently you are much busier than we are, especially as you say you are short of nurses. If Arnold does have an operation, hope he will get over it alright, let me know please. How is Riseborough, Mee & Betts going along, would you kindly remember me to them. I'd heard Sister Welch had left, but I didn't know where she had gone. You have no Sister on night duty with you now, there's only two of you on together isn't there, that means you are pretty busy in the morning. You see by the address that I am still in England, though a step nearer France. Am hoping to be here about a month, of course can't say, may only be here another week. Am glad to hear you've had no air raids; we've had two warnings since being here (24th) which meant us turning out for 2 hours at 11 o'clock. Not altogether pleasant, but we have good shelters in the form of tunnels underneath the castle on the cliffs. Did it keep fine so that you were able to write those 8 letters. Dover is very much like Plymouth, only not so good. The hills are much steeper and longer, there's one fault with it, that is, it takes so long to go home. Shall have to spend 2 out of the 4 days of my leave travelling, that's if I get any. We are allowed to go in town every night after the first few nights there isn't much to see.

Must now draw to a close as it's nearing post time.

yours Sincerely,

L. Sweetnam.

Much Spying Going On

11th June 1918

23593 C. Bay
16th R. Warwicks, B.E.F., France, Postmark Field Post Office
Passed by Censor 2494

(21 The Drive, Chingford, London, E.4.)

Dear Nurse,

Perhaps this may come as a little surprise to you, although you know I was likely to go at any time, yet you didn't know I had left England. We left England on the 2nd June, after having 6 days leave, time was so short at home, and we were very busy at Dover that I wasn't able to keep my promise. Since leaving England we haven't been in any one place longer than 2 days and it was only last night that we joined the battery, so you see, I haven't had much opportunity to write before. Probably you are aware that we are(not) allowed to put anything regarding military news, otherwise I should be able to tell you on what part of the line we are. On joining the batt. we were fortunate to find it out of the line, so now we are in billets and ours is in a barn by the side of a canal. We are not on the same front as I was last October, that (*sic*) was a little too warm to be comfortable, this place is none too cold though. There are still a few French inhabitants here, if the Fritz's come any nearer, they will have to clear out. It seems a shame to turn them out, but if they are left too near the line, they have to be watched very, very closely, otherwise there is much spying going on.

It's now teatime and as I have several more letters to write afterwards, must now close.

Will write Nurse Hawke in a day or so.

Yours sincerely,
L Sweetnam

How Long Will it Last?

4th July 1918

23593 16th R. Warwicks, B.E.F., France

(Passed by Censor 2494) On Active Service
Post mark Field Post Office 5 JY 18

21 The Drive, Chingford, London

Dear Nurse,

I was very pleased to receive your letter dated 19.06.18.

So sorry haven't been able to answer before, but have had very little time to write, the last day or so it has improved so I now take the opportunity whilst I have it. Don't suppose you will receive this much before the beginning of next week. When I read that sentence of yours "Nearly every boy we have in here at present will have to go out again worse luck." The thought past through my mind, "I wonder how much longer she thinks the war is going to last"? If it continues another month we shall be entering the 5th year. One can hardly believe it, but there it is, when will it end? Some think this year, others say the last 4 will be worse than the 1st 54, well I hope I'm not in the last 5. You can do what you like when on night duty I suppose, that's how you have such fine times. Wouldn't think I was very hard to wake up in the morning, Sister Dowler used to do that when she brought the tea around. I may say I was always awake but pretended to be asleep, perhaps that's why it seemed so hard to awake me. I'm glad to see you have still a few who are willing to give a helping hand.

Was surprised to hear of Sergt. Naylor being transferred to the R.E. I wonder if he will continue to stay at his old job. You think it doubtful if I shall hear from Sergt. Naylor before writing him, otherwise you would not have underlined "may." So far I haven't heard from him. At present I am on a Lewis Gun Course, what is commonly known with the Batt. As a scrounge – 14 days in all. It's a scrounge when the Batt. is in the line, but when they out, it isn't much of a one, seeing we are on parade until 4 p.m. and when the Batt out of line we have every afternoon to ourselves.

If you are enjoying the same kind of weather at Chingford as we are having, it must be splendid cycling to and from the Hospital.

Must now close.

Yours sincerely,   L. Sweetnam

On Very High Ground

19th August 1918

Sweetnam

C. Coy, 10 Plat. 16 R. Warwicks, B.E.F. France

Passed by Censor No 2494   Answered 19.8.18

Dear Nurse,

Very many thanks for letter dated 22.7.18. Was hoping to have answered before but have been too busy. Trust by now your brother has reached India safe and that you have heard from him. Hope he doesn't have the misfortune of being torpedoed this time. Thank you for reminding **Sergt. Naylor** have written him since and had a reply also 2 snapshots, one of the wards, both you and nurse Hawke are there, also a few of the old boys. Have quite a nice little collection of snapshots from Brookfield now, but still there's room for more. I wonder where Sister Witch is now, do you know. Bank holiday here was rather wet, Tuesday was very wet, yesterday and today has been better, though it's none too promising now but I hope it will keep fine until we have finished our rest, or at least done tracking. At present we are on very high ground and as we were coming off clothing parade, we could see for miles, could have spent the afternoon and evening very pleasantly with a field glass, fore there were many objects of interest in view.

My chum is ready to go out so must close.

Yours sincerely

L Sweetnam

Convoys for Convalescence

3rd September 1918

 Sweetnam

From: Pioneer Plot, 16thR Warwicks, B.E.F.
Passed by censor 6706
Stamped Field Post Office R5   05.09.18

Answered 11.09.18

Dear Nurse, _____

Yours sincerely Sorry haven't been able to answer you before, especially after receiving such a long and interesting letter. Probably you will be saying the same thing again "It's about time I heard from Sweetnam" now. But I don't suppose you will be on night duty.

I have been wondering if you will be having any of our boys in your next few convoys, if by any means you do, please let me know especially if they come from C Coy Though I suppose it's very unlikely but it's the unlikely that happens. Arnold is having a rather long stay; his stay is nearly as long as Coles isn't it? Hope your next letter will say he is now out of bed. Kindly remember me to him please and tell him men are wanted out here. Coles I think would be one which you would like back but not in the same condition.

Have often wondered who cleans your numerals and hat badge now or are cleaned by yourself now.

The weather has changed here during the past few days. It has been much cooler, especially of a night-time and also showery.

It's a glorious evening and most of us are all dressed up but nowhere to go. Have you ever been in that fix before, we often are out here.

Will now close, hoping when you can spare a few minutes to hear from you.,

L. Sweetnam

Our Hut

21st September 1918

Sweetnam

Army Post Office   B.E.F France
Passed by censor 6706
Miss D. Nicholas, 21 The Drive,
Chingford, London, E4

Dear Nurse,

For twice, I think you will not be on night duty, when receiving this, of course I can't say when you answer this that you won't be on night duty when you answer this for then you please yourself as to when you answer it. By now you will have nearly finished your fortnight on Theatre duty and I don't suppose you will be very sorry either, will you? Am glad to hear Arnold is now up and getting on fine. Ask him again if he won't come out here and help drive back the Huns if he can't use his rifle well then crutches will do.Sunday 22nd

Had to put this aside yesterday and seeing it is very quiet I will recommence. The wind has been blowing strong all day now its blowing a gale and it looks as though when the wind dies down a little we shall be having plenty of rain, in fact I believe it has started now.

In our hut we have made a wooden door and we have a bright wood fire burning in the centre so the weather is not troubling us much, although it must be very uncomfortable for the lads who are holding the line at present. This morning at 6.30 one of the men had the fire going and a canteen of coffee made which he passed around to the dozen who are in the hut and ever since then the fire has been burning. I believe Tony likes his fires and also his drop of tea after dinner and from my little experience nurses do as well.

The rain is now pouring down, but it's only a heavy shower, as it is now brightening for which I am thankful, it being teatime. The tea will soon be up and I shall have to issue it out to each man.

I wonder if Nurse Hawkes received my last letter safely, you saying she is on night duty made me think of it.   Must now close

   Yours sincerely.   L Cpl L. Sweetnam

The Boshe Have Left

1st November 1918

Sweetnam

From: Pioneer Plot, 16th R Warwicks, B.E.F.
Passed by censor 2494
Stamped Field Post Office 53   3 Nov 18
Answered 18.11.18

Dear Nurse,

Sorry to have kept you so long in waiting for a reply, now I am wondering if you are on night duty, seeing its nearly a month ago since I received yours, at any rate I should think by now you have finished Theatre duty and then its either morning or night duty.
I'm thinking it'll be a long time before we are in civies again even if peace was declared this week, it would be some months before we left France, it's possible though that I may be in them before Arnold. News certainly has been much better during the past month or so, but it isn't finished yet. There are a few civilians in this place where we are at present. The first day we were here (a few hours after the Bosh had left it) there were only about a dozen who were left behind, but since then many have returned from other parts.

Must now draw to a close.

Yours sincerely,
L. Sweetnam

ARNOLD

Figure 9 Arnold with Sister Welch

Figure 10 Arnold, Munro 'Roller' and Sergeant

Dorothy's note: 'It looks as though Arnold is recovering   enough to be able to use crutches'

Southwark Military Hospital

17th March 1918

F2 Ward, Southwark Military Hospital,
East Dulwich Grove,
London SE 22

Dear Nickie,

First of all I want to know what you mean by hoping I shan't mind you inflicting that letter on me as you put it. You know jolly well I shall always be glad to hear from you. It was jolly nice of you to be so concerned about me. One thing you didn't wish you could have the nursing of me more than I did. They looked after me alright but it was not like my two little "Angels."

Sorry to hear you don't like Whipps Cross very much but I'm not surprised.

As you can see I have arrived a Dulwich but only to find myself in the cart. They tell me Mr. Compton has gone and they are closing on the 31st. Aren't I lucky eh?

We are all going to Lewisham sometime next week, I believe and they advise me to get a transfer home from there which I shall probably do. The only thing against that of course is I believe they are closing down there too. I've written home to find out.

You might thank your mother very much for her kind message and tell her I certainly won't forget where you live if ever I happen to be in Chingford and I hope I shall someday. I should very much like to see you all again. Will let you know how I get on.

With kind regards,
Yours sincerely,   A. Arnold.

PS I'm sorry I'm so long answering but it was due to shifting. Now, mind, don't forget whenever you feel in the humour you write, because a letter from you will always be very welcome. AA

Author's note: Arnold addresses Dorothy as 'Nickie' probably because of her surname being Nicholas. It does make it sound familiar.

Lewisham Military Hospital

16th March 1919

Connaught Ward,
Lewisham Military Hospital,
London SE.

Dear Nickie,

I'm sorry to have left your letter unanswered so long but have been expecting to come here daily and eventually arrived on Monday. It is not too bad here, but I've been in better surroundings. I think that is about the best description of the place, I can give you. I think I shall have a try at getting boarded home as an out-patient as I'm getting sick of hospital life. The doctor here too, doesn't give one a lot of confidence. After looking at the wound yesterday he asked me if it was a fracture and if I had lost any bone. He is a civvie chap and old and I think it is about time he packed up. Now for a change of subject. You asked me in your letter if I was cross. No, my dear, I was not and never could be with you. Now I guess you wish you had me near you so as to set about me for that eh? By the way, your description of me as a good safety valve for bad temper etc. is very flattering, I don't think.

Hawkie tells me some of the Military part of Whipps Cross is closing down soon so I suppose you will be unemployed again. (Poor mother). I reckon you'll be wanting that safety valve again then.

With regard to those photos. Yes, I should like some very much if you could let me have them. And now I think I'll pack up. Will you please remember me to your mother and Mollie.

Cheerio, sincerely yours,

A. Arnold.

Cleverest Surgeon in London

16th May 1919

B. Ward, Military Hospital,
Pendell Street,
London W.C.2.

Dear Nick,

I'm almost ashamed to put pen to paper as I find by your letter it is just a month ago since you sent me those photos.

However I thank you very much for them and crave forgiveness at the delay. As you can see I've had another move as Lewisham has closed down now. I think this will be the last as I'm marked for a Board which sits on the 29th. I nearly got away this week but the doctor said she could not board me on crutches so put me off until the next one.

In the meantime I'm getting massage and being fixed up with a splint to enable me to walk with sticks then I shall be well away. Of course if they want me to continue the treatment I shall do so as I believe they are very clever here but I shan't press for it myself as I want to get out of it. I might mention they are all lady doctors here and the chief surgeon Dr. Garett Anderson is, I think, considered one of the cleverest surgeons in London. Although the treatment is good, the place is otherwise <u>rotten.</u> as they only let us out from 2 to 6 which doesn't go down very well after Brookfield. We also breakfast at 6.30 so you can guess that agrees with me top. I don't think. But there, I shouldn't be a soldier if I didn't do a bit of grousing, should I? One consolation, it won't last long before I go home I'll come over one day to see you, providing of course you are not too cross with me.

Yours sincerely,

A. Arnold.

> PS. How many cigarettes do you smoke a day now? I hope you and Hawkie don't compare notes as the two letters are practically identical.

*Author's note: Dr. **Louisa Garrett Anderson**, CBE (28 July 1873 – 15 November 1943) was a medical pioneer, a member of the Women's Social and Political Union, a suffragette, and social reformer. When the First World War broke out, she and Flora Murray founded the Women's Hospital Corps (WHC), and recruited women to staff it. Believing that the British War Office would reject their offer of help, and knowing that the French were in need of medical assistance, they offered their assistance to the French Red Cross. The French accepted their offer and provided them the space of a newly built hotel in Paris as their hospital. Anderson became the chief surgeon.*

In January 1915, casualties began to be evacuated to England for treatment, she returned to work for the Royal Army Medical Corp and was involved in the treatment of almost 50,000 soldiers between May 1915 and September 1919. She was also involve in pioneering a new method of treating septic wounds. Arnold was treated during 1918 and post war 1919.

BETTS

Nineteen Months in Hospital

2nd May 1918

Ward A, Military Hospital,

Colchester

Dear Nurse Nicholas,

I am very sorry that I was unable to come over to Chingford to say good-bye but time was short and the trains were all upside down. Still I will come over and see you as soon as I leave this wicked place, little did I think that when I said goodbye to you yesterday morning that I was off to Colchester that day. Well Nurse, we thought of you last night taking the tea round to one or two of the boys. It is a thing that one does not see here. Never mind, better days in store, I hope. Dear nurse, I am very glad that I gave you that Box on Tuesday as it was the last night. I had thought of keeping it till Saturday. I only wish that I could have given you more for you have been far too good to me the 5 months I spent at Brookfield. They are the best 5 months I have spent in my 19 months of Hospital life and I have only you and Nurse Hawke to thank for making it so happy and comfortable for me.

Well Dear Nurse, I must now come to a close but will write you again as soon as I hear how I get on with my Board.

Thanking you once more for your kindness.

Accept my kindest regards.

Yours sincerely, Betty.

Figure 11 Dorothy centre with 'Betty'

Waiting for 'The Board'

12th May 1918

Ward A, Military Hospital,
Colchester,
 Sunday
Dear Nurse Nicholas (Nicky),

Well, nurse, Dick and I are still here waiting every day for the news to come through for us both to go for our Board (better late than never). Ellis had his Board yesterday but did not get his discharge. They told him that he could do Police Duty so he is very disappointed. He is off for 10 days leave on Wednesday but will not be able to call and see you all at the Hospital as time will be very short. Dear Nurse, you lucky girl to win the whist drive prize then Friday's night off. How did you manage it. Just luck I suppose. How is Mr. Hawke going on? I hope he is much better than he was last time I heard of him. Thank God when we get away from this awful place if it was not for waiting to see the result of the next few days we would not stop here another day. For one thing, food is (rotten) and that is saying a lot. Give us good old Brookfield again. Still better days are in store, I hope.

Well, Nicky, I will write you again as soon as I hear result of the Board.

Dick, Ellis and myself send our kindest regards and best wishes to yourself and all the nurses – also to Sgt Naylor and Arnold.

Write and let us know all the news about Brookfield.

 Goodbye-e-e

Yours sincerely,

Arthur Betts (Betty)

COLE

Essex Convalescent Home

23rd November 1917

Essex Convalescent Home,
Clacton on Sea, Essex.

Answered
30.11.17

Dear Nurse,

As promised I am writing to let you know we arrived safely. Pleased to tell you we are settling down nicely. This is quite a nice place and everyone here is very good and kind. After being at Brookfield so long I was very sorry to come away. But all good things come to an end and one cannot be content to spend their whole life in hospital. There is consolation in the knowledge that this is a step nearer home. I am longing to get home again. I heard from my sister this morning glad to say she is going on nicely also her little boy, who is to be called Ronald Arthur. I am proud to think I am an uncle. I am just longing to see him. Please accept my sincere thanks nurse for all you have done for me and I am most grateful to you all. I know I was a great trouble for a long time. I shall never forget the kindness of all at Hale End. Since our arrival I seem to have done nothing else but write letters. Still, I have many to write. This place is about twenty minutes' walk from the sea front. I was surprised to find Worral and Sadler still here. Worrall has his wife and three little boys down here with him. He is allowed out until 9.30 p.m.

Please give my kindest regards to little Mollie and your people.

I remain, your sincerely,

Arthur Cole.

Figure 12 Mr. Compton, Matron and COLE

IRVINE

Private William G. Irvine DIED 11 JAN 1919. He was an American who joined the Royal Warwickshire Regiment, and he was awarded the Victory and The British War Medal   **14021**

Irvine was a friend of the Nicholas family from their time living in Brooklyn USA and had been sent to Europe to join the war effort. He was also married. Bill, or Billie as he was called by his family, was the brother of Connie who went to school with Dorothy. Connie wrote Dorothy to say he had gone directly to France and his address was *Private William G Irvine, Co, "A" 104th Machine Gun Battalion , American Expeditionary Forces in France.*

In Connie's letter to Dorothy dated 11th July 1918, she says the following: *By the way I gave him your address but he landed in France. He says everything is alright but that it is a long way from home. In the papers the other day, I noticed that they said his division was near the Front just waiting orders to go in. When I think of all of us as little kids in Bensonhurst, this muddle seems to be a dream. But out of all this mess a safer era will be made so that the little children now playing 'tap on the back' will have a more carefree and happier future to live through. It does make one proud to think that every one of our playmates are in it or ready to go into it.*

Hoping the Hun Will Cry 'Quits'

23rd October 1918   *Answered 1.11.18*

14201

Passed by Censor 6095
W.G. Irvine, US Army – Soldiers Mail
Soldiers' Christian Association – On Active Service – S.C.A Camp
Home.

To Miss Dorothy Nicholas,
21 The Drive,
Chingford, London, England. Answered 1.11.18

Dear Dorothy,

Your letter reached me yesterday with a lot of home mail. Have been
in a convalescent camp since October 3 and am leaving today for
Bushey a rest camp, I think. Have certainly had a nice stay here and
am fit again. Glad you heard from Jack. Connie wrote that she
expects to be over before very long. Think also there is a good chance
of *Ruts* arriving before long. We have been giving the Hun a bit of the
right stuff lately and am hoping he will soon cry quits as that is the
only way he will have peace now I think. Have been near Rouen and
it is the first good signal place I've been near since arriving. Has been
quite a nice change. There is a rumour that they may give us a leave
to England. Hope it is more than a rumour as I am anxious to see
England and all you people. Wonder if I would know you after so long.
Must get ready to run now so will close.

Remember me to the rest of the family.   Bill   Oct 23

Author's note: 'Ruts' was a friend of Bill, also called 'Ruttie.'

October 1918
Soldiers' Christian Association
On Active Service paper.

Dear Mrs. Nicholas   (*Dorothy's mother*)

I am now in a war convalescent tent camp No. 2. Company having been hit with a small piece of shrapnel and expect I will be here for a week or more yet. Was glad to hear from you. Mail means a lot to us out here especially as it takes so long for home letters to arrive.

We are all cheerful over the news lately and are hoping the war will soon end and that we may go home again. Expect it can't last so very much longer now.

So Jack is in the Navy. Hope he likes it. I prefer the army. I really had enough of water coming over here. Seems ages since I landed and it has only been a bit over four months.

Was kind of sorry didn't get a good cure while I was about it so as to see Blighty but am duly thankful I didn't 'go west' as I sure do want to see the States and home again.

It's very pleasant here and quite a rest from the live Movies and entertainments and a large city altho (*sic*) I haven't' seen it as yet and hope to before I leave here. Can't think exactly of your address but I think I have it right. Remember me to Mr. Nicholas and Dorothy, also Jack when you write him.

William
W. G Irvine, MG W.S.A.

WAGSTAFF

Both letters from A. Wagstaff do not give his full name nor his military number so, unfortunately, no further records have been found.

Military Heart Hospital

19th February 1918

A Wagstaff, Ward F2,
Military Heart Hospital,
Sobraon Barracks,
Colchester, Essex.

Dear Miss Nicholas,

Thanks so very much for your letter which I have just received. Yes I know who you are, can I forget you after all you did for me whilst I was their (sic), I have to thank you all very much, things are very much the same here and I am afraid they will always be so, as there is no one to get them altered, I have got more used to the place, got into the tune of things, so I can now settle down for six long weeks, perhaps more.

I can just picture major with the confetti. I have a good idea who put it in the bed (and you would be one) and the other Nurse Armstrong.

Sorry to hear about Sgt Naylor not being so well, and I hope he will soon be quite alright again as he is in the right hospital for a quick recovery. I feel very much better now, quite different than I did the first few days here, but as for me liking Colchester, that will never be, as I had quite enough of the place when we were training here 1916 & 1917. We left here to go to France, hoping the never to see the place again, but just my luck I have landed here again. One thing, it is far better than France and the longer they keep me here the longer I shall be away from France, but after being in a place like Hale End, then finding yourself here is quite a difference, I also got a letter from Sister Dowler so I will write back this afternoon.

I was glad you did not get 28 days C.B over your court martial for they might have sent you down to this hospital for 28 days, the sister here said yesterday the sooner she got away from here the better she would like it, so it is not only the men what dislikes the place. We can hear the guns firing at Fritz at nights when he is over and they say he dropped a bomb very close to here on Sunday night, he should have lit this ward, we might have got a move then. Well nurse, please excuse me writing with black lead as I cannot get the ink yet as it is in use, I think this is all the news for a while, so with closing again thank you very much for your letter.

Sincerely yours,

Wagstaff

Figure 13 Sobraon Barracks Military Hospital

Mustard Leaf Treatment

9th March 1918

A. Wagstaff
F2 Military Heart Hospital,
Sobraon Barracks, Colchester

Dear Nurse,

Many thanks for your letter dated 6.3.18 which I received this morning. Yes, I am very glad my term is drawing to a close in this hospital. I hope they don't keep me longer than 6 weeks as three already sent here has looked more like months than weeks. They keep sending me out but there is always others to fill the beds, they even send men from Scotland here, it is such a nice place, I thought last night old Fritz was coming as a patient for he was very near, he must have known what sort of a place it was as he p assed on his way, I never heard the guns so plainly as last night. It just reminded me of **Hale End** only we are not as near the guns in Colchester. Glad to hear Betts is pulling round his operation and hope he will soon be able to get about without the aid of crutches.

I am now on what they call the heart treatment and after a fortnight's drill I feel no better, they gave me a mustard leaf yesterday and I had to keep it on for over half an hour, and I knew about it. I don't want anymore, they will break your heart here, not cure it.

I had a letter from Bob Munro and he told me about the billiard matches, I think Bartle will be the winner as they said he was a very good player.

We are having grand weather down here but the place spoils all the enjoyment. There is no pleasure going out.

I think this is all for a while so will close sending very best wishes to all.

Sincerely yours,   Wagstaff.

*A **mustard plaster** is a poultice of mustard seed powder spread inside a protective dressing and applied to the chest or abdomen to stimulate healing. In times past and present, the mixture was spread onto a cloth and applied to the chest or back. The mustard paste itself should never make contact with the skin. Applied externally, black mustard is used in the treatment of bronchial pneumonia and pleurisy.*

Mustard oil irritates mucous membranes; therefore, excessive internal use has been known to cause stomach problems and kidney irritation. Breathing the vapours of a mustard plaster can trigger sneezing, coughing, asthma attacks, or eye irritation. Leaving a mustard plaster on the bare skin for too long will lead to burning, blisters, or potentially even ulcers.

COCKBURY

Private J. W. Cockbury was in the 62nd T.R. Battalion, Category C2, Training Reserve.

Figure 14 Letter Heading YMCA with HM Forces

Not Getting Proper Treatment

January 1917   *Answered 14/2/17*

Pte J. W. Cockbury   Reg No. 21450
8 Hut, No. 1 Camp, H. Company,
62nd Training Reserve Batt
Kinsnel Park, Denbighshire.

Dear Nurse Nicholas,

Just a line to let you know how I am getting on, of course you will see that I am not at Liverpool. I went there and stayed about 10 days, then they sent me to await a Board. That I think will put me on home service. I had rather a rough time at L. Pool. My cough returned as bad as ever and I could not get any proper treatment. I was glad to get sent from their (*sic*). I am improving now.

By the way, have you heard from Nurse Manger? When you write her, ask her does she carry a half crown in her pocket to stand on. Well Nurse, I hope you receive this small note all right and that you are keeping in good health. Remember me to Nurse Bush, Hawkes, Armstrong and any others who would be pleased to hear about me. I now close these few lines and remain Yours Truly.
            Ptt. J. Cockbury.

            ....Late Kitchen Maid and Stoker!

Being Transferred

25th August 1918

Pte J. W. Cockbury 21450
8 Hut, No. 1 Camp, H. Company,
62nd Training Reserve Batt
Kinsnel Park, Denbighshire.

Dear Nurse Nicholas,

Many thanks for your kind letter. I was very pleased to hear from you but sorry to hear that your sister has been laid up. I hope that she has fully recovered by the time you receive these few lines.

I daresay you will be glad to get back to Hospital again. I hope to hear better news of Wallace next time you write. I really thought as he had gone to Bath as the morning I came away he drew his kit out to go away. I think it rather hard lines for poor Nurse Manger having gone to such a hard place, I hope they will soon find out her capabilities and mover her further up into the Nursing Ward, for I am sure she is more fit than a good many of the nurses I have met in Military Hospitals. Well Nurse, I am pleased to tell you as I am feeling much better than when I wrote last, my cough is much better. I have been before a Board and my Category is C2 and I have been transferred to the 62nd I.B. Battalion, as you will see I have a number and Company so mind you put the new address. I am pleased to say that the change in the weather has done me good and I am living in hope of the fine days so I can feel my old self again.

Now I think as I have told you all the news this time again and hoping at these few lines find you in the best of health.

I close with regards to yourself and any others of the Nurses who may ask after me, hoping to remain yours truly,

21450 Pte J. W. Cockbury.

P.S. I will write Nurse Manger this week.

PURDY

Reg. No. 121916

Private Bertie Henry Purdy

Enlisted 26th August 1914 in the Tank Corps (Machine Gun Corps)

Discharged 23rd June 1918 – No longer physically fit for war service.

Born in 1899. Died in Ilford, Essex in 1950. He was in the Machine Gun Corps

Figure 15 Bertie H Purdy Military Info

One of the Boys

25th August 1918

Answered 26.8.18

Pte. Bertie H. Purdy   121916
G.G.C.
Convalescent Home
Upminster, Essex

Dear Nurse

Just a few lines to let you know how things are going on and what kind of a place this is. This place is a little mission hall with about 20 beds in it and when I first saw it I thought if we had walked into a barn or rag shop by mistake. We all went for a walk around the village and saw all there was to see in about five minutes, there were about 20 houses and half a dozen shops. I have never seen such a dreary place in all my life what with being next to a cemetery and going all day without seeing a girl, though that seems to trouble Ward more than me and anyone else. I have just seen Ward's letter to you and I think he is about right when he says I have got the hump. I have got it properly and no mistake.

I think the doctor comes round today so I am going to ask him to mark me out if he will so you can expect to see me down at Brookfield sometime next week. Remember me to Sergeant Naylor and Arnold and ask him how he likes his job of doing the hall.

Please excuse short letter as I don't feel like writing now.
I remain one of the boys

B Purdy

The Quarter-bloke

2nd October 1918

Pte B Purdy 121916
5th Batt 29 Coy
C7 Hut M Lines
MGC
Belton Park
Grantham   *Answered 7.10.18*
and 23.12.18

Dear Nicky,

I was very glad to receive your letter yesterday, and thanks for the tip about the leave but I am afraid you are a bit late because I had already heard about it and have applied for a leave. I will not be able to know wether (sic) they will grant me it as I am back at Harrowby Camp on an anti-aircraft course for 10 days and if they are going to let me have it I shall have to wait until I re-join my company.

I am glad you like the photo but I did not know that there were two that I had sent you. It must have been because it was getting dark when I put them in.

You can give the other one to any one you like if you can find anybody that would like it, and I should like to have a photo of you if you will be so good as to send me one.

I see that you are getting plenty of new men now, but fancy the quarter-bloke (as you call him), going. I don't know how you will manage now and convalescent too. Are his nerves still bad?

I should like to sit in a cold theatre all afternoon what is the matter with it, it would just suit me especially if you were there as well, you want to sit in a cold hut and listen to an officer spouting a lot of rot about aeroplanes and how to bring them down when they now (sic) about as much about it as I did and that's nothing at all.

Fancy you breaking Matron's pet teapot. I can just imagine Nicky get the wind up when it happened and having a bust up with Bridget I didn't think you could have a row with anyone. I should like to have seen you. I didn't have the luck to see anything like that happen while was there.

I think this is all at present so Good-bye

I remain
>yours Sincerely
>>B Purdy

Author's note: It seems that Dorothy had to deal with some very disturbed young men. Perhaps the 'quarter-bloke' suffered from psychological trauma.

HOWARD

Cpl B Howard

On Returning to the Army

3rd May 1918

33433 Cpl B. Howard, No. 5 Coy
K.R.R.C. R.G.A. Barracks, Sheerness.
5th May 1918   BERT HOWARD

Dear Nurse,

At last I take the opportunity of writing you as promised. I trust you are keeping well as I am pleased to say this leaves me in the pink. So far I have done little other than travel about since I returned to the Army. First of all I went to Winchester and went from there to Salisbury Plain. There I was marked 'unsuitable' and sent here. For the present I have been given temporary category B3 pending a Medical Board which is due here this week. I have quite an easy time being in Barracks fairly comfortable. The food is very good and considering the times rather plentiful. I continue to keep in touch with Hospital work for I have on two occasions been in charge of the guard in the detention ward at the Military Hospital here. There is (*sic*) six patients, three of which are subject to fits, the other three are prisoners. One attempted suicide by cutting his rist(*sic*) in seven places. He will of course lose the use of his hand.

I have had a letter from Cpl Stedman he was at Ripon and awfully fed up with the place. All he seemed to look forward to was his leave which he said he would spend with me at Walthamstow if possible. I wrote Sergeant Naylor last Monday acknowledging the receipt of the snapshots. I have not heard from him up to the present. Kindly tell him I will let he know the result of my Board. I am very pleased to have your photograph. It will always be a pleasure and revive happy memories of the days I spent at Brookfield.

Give my kind regards to nurses Hake, Matheson, Randall and Armstrong. Also to any of the boys that are left.

Remember me kindly to your parents and sister.
I sincerely hope they are keeping well.
I will now conclude withal good wishes and kindest regards from..
Yours very Sincerely, ,

Bert Howard.

Had His Ticket

10th June 1918

33433 Cpl B. Howard,
No 5 Coy K.R.R.C.
R.G.A Barracks, Sheerness.

Dear Nurse

I am sorry I have not answered your letter before. However I hope this will find you in the best of health. I had hopes that I should have found an opportunity of calling at the hospital before this. I expect you heard through some of the patients that I was home a few weeks ago. At that time I was doing escorts. Unfortunately I have been taken off that and now I just do guards and go in charge of the fatigue parties. It was a pity for on my next journey to London I intended to call at the Hospital.

My parents had a narrow escape Whit Sunday night. A bomb dropped within a few yards of the house shattering all the windows and doing considerable damage in the house. Happily nobody was injured and the damage is covered by insurance. I applied for a few days leave without success. However should I not get away before I shall be entitled to five days in a month's time.

I am going before a Board one day this week and hope to get discharged, unless I hope I retain my present category. Vis BIII. I have a letter from Woolwich Arsenal saying they have applied to the War Office for my services. The application has not come through the Battalion yet so I am just carrying on from day to day patiently waiting.

I sincerely hope Dick, Betts, Reggie, Arnold and Mee get their tickets. I am glad the boys take kindly to the new Sister and hope she will be happy and comfortable at "Brookfield." I must now close. Remember me kindly to Nurses Hawke, Redmall and Matheson, also Sgt Naylor. Give my kind regards to your parents and sister. I sincerely trust they are keeping well.

Best wishes and kindest regards from Yours Very Sincerely,

B. Howard.

Note by Dorothy on back of letter dated 17.7.18 'Heard from Arnold that Cpl Howard had his ticket so did not answer this as don't know his address.'

DOWLER, Mary

Nursing Sister who was an ex-colleague of Dorothy's and worked in another hospital.

Mount Hospital, Faversham, Kent

8th May 1918   *Answered*
12.5.18

Dear Nurse Nicholas,

At last my promised letter. Was waiting until I would feel settled down in my new abode. I trust you all are quite well at Brookfield. Have thought of you many times. I expect a lot of the boys are marked out, that's I Knew how Mclud my 'Little Bell' Hippard and how is Risborough and Arnold? Well, I had a very nice little rest, had almost a fortnight, quite unexpected but my experience at Tunbridge Wells where I went first was anything but pleasant. Very ..ish and really it all seemed like a dream and in fact it does still. I found I had one VAD (40 beds). and she had a tremendous amount of extra work to do, including black leading grate, sweeping etc. Incidentally the Comdnt did not approve of my speaking to her about it and said my manner was very hostile. I helped the VAD in every way and she told the Comdnt I did not help her and she slept 4 hours one night on the couch while I went quietly round!! Amazing in one sense, don't you think? It was the first time they had a sister on night there so I suppose I must overlook it, but at the same time the lie (can call it nothing else) of the Nurse hurt me very much indeed. But I was relieved to get away. Nothing mattered. The comdnt reported me as very disagreeable at the Headquarters!! So I got it from all quarters!!! but her wows did not have much effect for they told her it was the first time they had a word said against me. They were very nice and just when I interviewed and told me to think no more of it and sent me here on Tuesday but still it is very humiliating and my first experience of the sort and I hope the last.

This is a nice Hospital (50 beds). Am sleeping here so no Lantern walks! for which I am thankful. Have a dear little room and a lovely vista. We have just the two sisters and we take alternate day and night monthly. We have entire charge. They just reopened on Tues last. Had 4 men when I arrived, from a Local Camp, and on Thurs we had a convoy of 39 and on Friday 8 so we are busy, plenty to do. Nearly all wounded and some very badly gassed. All the men have been in the big push and had one night in Chatham before coming here. I have two VADs on light and one orderly. The nurses have no washing up to do. No extra work.....a Contrast from Tunbridge Hells!!

Send my love to Hawkes. I did not say goodbye to her but I knew she understood. Kind remembrances to the boys whom I knew. Shall often think of Brookfield. Am sure you are all glad to have Matron back.

Goodnight, with love and kindest remembrances,

yours sincerely,

Mary E. Dowler.

Author's Note: The Mount Hospital was a large 18th century house at Ospringe on the south-western edge of Faversham in Kent. It was used as a hospital during the First World War and is now residential apartments. Although 1918 was the end of the First World War, most hospitals for the wounded did not close until 1919 or later.

FRED

Figure 16 Frederick Hugh Nicholas 1894-1915

Dorothy's Cousin

Private FREDERICK HUGH "FRED" NICHOLAS

Theatre of War 9th Battalion Welsh Regiment. He was born on the 15th December 1894 in Neath, Glamorgan and became a private Reg No 13460. His father, Hugh, was 47 and his mother, Elizabeth, was 31. He had three sisters. He died on December 21, 1915, in Flanders, France and was buried in Saint-Venant, Pas-de-Calais, France. 'Appendicitis' stated on war record.

From letters to my grandmother, who was Frederick's cousin, I learn that he joined in about October 1914 and died on the 21st December 1915, six days after his 22nd birthday. He had been attending college in Cardiff before joining the war effort. He told Dorothy in some detail about life in the trenches, the French countryside, what they were expecting the outcome to be and his hopes. He also mentioned what it was like when the King and Lord Kitchener visited the regiments in training.

At the age of 17, Fred was an apprentice joiner and living with his parents at 14 Lewis Road, Neath, Glamorgan, Wales. His father Hugh was a joiner for the Railway Company

His last letter in my possession was in mid-September 1915 so we have about 2 months missing before he died. However a few more letters written to his friend Ben cover the rest of the year leading to his death.

Fred refers often to Mollie who was Dorothy's little sister and would have been aged about five when the letters were written.

Pre-war at University in Cardiff

9 Angus St.,
Roath Park
Cardiff

Dear Dorothy,

Just a line to let you know that I have not forgotten you all. You will see by the above that I am now at Cardiff. I have been here a fortnight and have only one more week before I go back to Neath to 'Work'

I think that the last I heard of you was that you were going away for a change. I hope by now you are in the best of health again. Are you coming to visit us at Neath this summer? Shall be very pleased to see you anytime. How is Jack getting on? I should like to hear from him when he can spare time to write. He ought to have had enough of work by now. Phyllis is at Cosheston and Doris and Dad are joining her there this week. Doris still keeps well. She has been in Kilgetty this last fortnight. How is your Mother and Father? And how is Wee Mollie? Quite a big girl now I suppose. I should like to see you all again soon, but I don't suppose I shall this year anyhow. **What with the war and all the other things. Isn't this an awful world, nothing but "Wars and rumours of wars." I have offered myself to the Royal Engineers but have not yet been called up and believe me I am not in a hurry to.** I am nearly killed with work up here in the University. Nothing but work, all day and nearly all day (sic). I passed the place where you lived when you were in this city 'Ruthen Gardens.' It is close to the college. That's all now. Hoping that you are by this time in the best of health and all the others as well. With best love to all,

I remain

your Sincere Cousin

Fred -

xxxx to . I will send her a P.C. next week. F.

The King and Lord Kitchener Visit

Oct 1st, 1914

9th Batt. Welsh Regl. B Coy
c/o YMCA, Parkhouse Camp
Salisbury Plain

Dear Dorothy

Thanks very much for your letter which I received this morning. Very glad that you are all well, and that the war has not frightened you. We are having a jolly time here, plenty of work and plenty of food, of a sort. As you say we are getting rather tired of stewed meat and potatoes, but we also getting used to bread and cheese or jam. Margarine is counted as a luxury, which is very scarce. We haven't had any this week. But for all this we are very happy. I have had my "Karki" but most of them have not yet. It is comical to see them walking about with only one leg to a trouser, or with their shirt hanging out behind. The king passed here last Tuesday. We lined the road for him to pass. Lord Kitchener was with him. They didn't get out of the car. I suppose they thought we were not worth seeing. Anyhow they were called some nice things. I don't know how long we shall remain here. I think it will only be for a fortnight. We may get sent abroad in about 2 months, of course not to the front. We are supposed to be ready for the front after 6 months training. We have had one month, so we are not soldiers yet. I have just heard from home. They are all well there. Very sorry that I did not remember 's birthday. She must be a big girl by this time. I haven't had my photo taken in uniform yet when I have it will send you one. Only you mustn't laugh when you see it. I suppose Jack is too young to join. All the chaps from Neath have joined. There are close on 200 in our Camp alone. We were about 12,000 small caps to the men. They can't get 'Kaki.' Thanks very much for your offer to send some cakes. I am sure they would be very acceptable up here. I have had several from home also from Aunt Mary. We have plenty of socks for the present. I have three pairs of woollen ones.

I hope you will excuse this scribble. We have a holiday this afternoon but we have a sham fight from 6.30 to 9.30 p.m. tonight so we are having a rest. We were out from 8 o'clock until 12.30 this morning so you see we are kept busy. Very glad that Jack has plenty of work. Tell him to write to me. I would like to hear from him. I sent you a P.C. to Scotland in reply to your letter. Did you receive it. We are not certain of our letters reaching their destination, nor of receiving those sent to us. I have received all that has been sent to me. Well that's about all this time. Hope to hear from you again when you have time. Give my best to your father, mother, Jack and wee Mollie and accept same yourself from

Yours Sincerely

Fred 'x'

'x' Private F. H. Nicholas Not yet Col.

Still Under Canvas

31st October 1914
13460
B Company
9th Service Batt
Welsh Regt.
Parkhouse Camp
Salisbury Plain

Dear Dorothy,

I have time at last to answer your letter which I was very pleased to receive. Very glad that you are all well and that the war has not worried you very much. I am sure the Kaiser would run away if he heard threats and I also pity him if our chaps here get hold of him. We seem to be getting the better of the fighting at last and I think that it is only a matter of time. I don't think that we will be wanted in Germany, more likely to S. Africa or India. We will be ready to go abroad on Jany 1st and we are to have furlough any time before or at Xmas. I think we will be allowed 14 days. So I am looking forward to a holiday. Although we have had a fine time up here, I am anxiously waiting to get home again. We are still under canvas but we are building huts for ourselves and I hope they will soon be ready because we are having rough weather up here, and the place is in an awful mess. We are over the top of our boots in mud, but all the same I am enjoying myself. We have plenty of fun and we have a decent lot of chaps in the tent, so we have nothing to grumble at.

We go through the "physical torture" you spoke of, but there is no need to be sorry for me as I like that part of our work. It is much better than forming fours and platoons.

They are all well at home. One of my friends went home last week and he called at our house. I have nothing much to say this time. Nothing ever happens here out of the ordinary. Every day is the same and the best day is pay day.

Give my love to your Mother, Father, and Jack and accept same from your Cousin

Fred//

PS. I enclose a letter to F//

Awaiting Orders

October or November **1914**

Reg No 13460
B. Company 9th Battalion
Welch Regt.
Parkhouse Camp
Salisbury Plain

Sunday

Dear Auntie   - (Dorothy's mother)

I was very sorry that I was unable to visit you yesterday, but, as I said in my telegram, I couldn't get leave from our Colonel. All leave was stopped last Friday, as we are awaiting orders from the War Office to leave here at any minute. I hoped to get special permission just for a week and I didn't know until two o'clock yesterday that I had failed to obtain this. I was very disappointed indeed. I have been looking forward all last week to seeing you all again, but of course, I am a soldier now and   must put up with these sorts of things.

We hope to leave here very soon. All of us have severe colds and there are sure to be some deaths if we don't move quickly. One of our boys was taken to Tidworth Hospital a week ago with pneumonia, but the is getting better. Another of us went home Friday discharged. He had been in hospital for eight weeks with Rheumatism. It is awful to hear the boys coughing in the night here. I am very lucky I haven't had anything serious as yet. I had a bad cold last week, but I am glad to say that I am a lot better now although my throat is very sore.

We, who are on the huts are likely to stay here to finish them, while the rest of the Regt. goes away, but I do hope they will take us with them as I have had enough of Salisbury Plain for the rest of my life. We have no idea where we will be sent, it may be nearer London, if so I hope to be able to see you yet. Don't be surprised if I turn up some Saturday. I won't write next time and then you won't be disappointed. Tell Dorothy I am sorry I couldn't escort her to Church today. If it is anything like the same weather as we have with you its better sitting by the fire as it is pouring rain and the wind is blowing nicely.

Very sorry that is not well. I do hope she is better by this time. Ask her if she knows anyone on the enclosed P.C. We had it taken Saturday. We are going to have a better one taken shortly. I will send you another one. The boy on the left with the loaf was coming with me. He has friends in Walthamstow. The both of us had talked a lot of this visit.

Well that's all I have to say this time. Thank Jack for his letter. I will answer it shortly. Hoping that this will find you all quite well. With best love to Uncle, Dorothy, and Jack and also to yourself.

I remain   Your affectionate nephew

Fred   xxxxxxx

Waiting in Weston-Super-Mare

01 Feb 15

1 Manilla Crescent
Birnbeck Road,
Weston-Super-Mare

Dear Dorothy,

I have been thinking of writing to you for this last fortnight or more but have been putting it off until I cannot put it off any longer. We have been in this lovely place now nearly three weeks and we are having a fine time. The weather is lovely if it was not quite so cold. It would be just like summer and if it was not for our uniform we would think we were here on holiday.

We are staying in a big house on the Promenade. There are three of us staying here and we have very comfortable rooms and the best food, so you will see that being a s soldier in this town is all right. There are about 10 Regiments here now about 11,000 troops so we are a fine lot and the town is full up.

I don't know how long we shall remain here. I don't think they will let us be comfortable very long. There is talk about that we won't go out until the end of March, but we haven't heard anything officially. I heard from home last Saturday. They are quite well three. I hope you are all in the best of health. I haven't heard anything about you all for a very long time. I think I heard that Jack is better. I do hope he is and that he will have good health in the future.

That's all now I think. When you have some time to spare (which I know is not often as you are such a busy person) write and let me know how you all are. Give my love to your Father, Mother, Jack & and accept same from

Yours Sincerely

Fred -//-

General Smith-Dorrien, King and Kitchener

17th February 1915

1 Manilla Crescent,
Birnbeck Road,
Weston-Super-Mare

(Letter addressed to Miss D.M. Nicholas, 'Rusholme,' 21 the Drive, Chingford, Essex.)

Dear Dorothy,

I wrote to you a week ago and thought that I had posted it but I found it yesterday in my writing pad. I was very glad to hear through Aunt Mary yesterday that your Mother was better. I was very sorry for you all when I heard that she was ill and especially for you seeing that you had all the work to do. But of course a little work won't hurt you. I would have liked to have seen you when you had to get up at five. Isn't it nice to be able to stay in bed until 7.30. We have to be on parade at 8.30. We are to be vaccinated this week and then we will be ready for the front. Some of the other Regts here (we are 10,000 in town) are having 3 days leave so I hope to be home again very soon. I am trying to get my transfer to the Engineers but I don't think they will let me go. We are in the second new army under **Gen Smith-Dorrien** and we are supposed to go out in March. We march on an average over 20 miles a day so we are fairly tired at night. It has been raining today and we have had a holiday. The first since we've been here. There is a lot of talk that the **King and Kitchener are coming here next week**. I hope they won't as it will mean us standing about all day. Has your cousin Jack gone out yet?

That's all this time. Hoping that you are all now in the best of health. With best love to you all, I remain, yours sincerely

Fred -//-

*General **Sir Horace Lockwood Smith-Dorrien**, GCB GCMG DSO ADC (26 May 1858 – 12 August 1930) was a British soldier.*

In the spring of 1915 he commanded British Second Army at the Second Battle of Ypres. He was relieved of command by French for requesting permission to retreat from the Ypres Salient to a more defensible position.

Vaccinated Yesterday

19th March 1915

1 Manilla Crescent,
Birnbeck Rd.,
Weston-Super-Mare

Dear Dorothy,

I see by your last letter that you wrote to me on Feb 24th. It is now the above date and as I have no excuse for keeping you so long, I will not offer any. I heard from Aunt Mary that Jack's firm won't give him permission to join. Tell him not to be disappointed as if he joined now he would never see the war. The 9th Welsh are going to finish that or get finished. We had orders a fortnight ago to leave for Tidworth Barracks but they were cancelled owing to an outbreak of fever. The orders now are that we leave here for **Perham Downs** the end of this month. This is the place where we spent such a happy Xmas and I suppose will also spend Easter.

Very glad that your Mother is better although she could have been through another bout by this. But better late than never. Very sorry that you have not been favoured with an illness. You ought to be in Kitchener's. You would soon have something to go sick with. We were vaccinated yesterday. This is another of the privileges of being a soldier. Then my chum went to the Doctors with the toothache this morning so of course I had to go with him. I had a bad cold so the Doctor gave us the day off. This is another of the privileges.

I heard from home this week. Doris is laid up with the "Flu." I haven't heard if she is better. There doesn't seem any sign of the war ending does there? I have been a "Soldier" now for nearly 7 months. Doesn't time fly? And I am not getting younger. I was 21 last Monday so don't forget that I am a Man.

That's all now. Will write again soon. Best love to Uncle Aunt Jack & yourself.

from Fred //-

No talk yet of us going

24th April 1915

1 Manilla Crescent
Birnbeck Rd
Weston-Super-Mare

Dear Dorothy,

I don't know whose turn it is to write but I think it is mine, if not I will let you off with a caution. We are still in this delightful place, but I don't think we will be here very long. There are only three batts here now and one of these is leaving for the Plains on Monday. But we cannot grumble as we have had a good holiday during our three months stay here. There is no talk of us going to the front. I think Kitchener has forgotten the 9th Welsh, although of course we are in no hurry to go out.

Since I wrote last I have been home for a few days. I was home the Sunday after Easter. I had a very decent time the only fault that the time was so short. Doris has had a bad attack but I am glad to say that she was a lot better when I saw her, but she was still very weak. Dad & Phyllis were quite well. Phyllis was at Cosheston for a week at Easter. They were all well there. Uncle Tom from Pontyfrydd was down with us the weekend and I was home. He was having a holiday. I think he was going on to Cosheston after. How are you all at Chingford? Has Jack got over his disappointment? Have you had the pleasure of an illness yet? We may get moved back to the Plains shortly. If so I hope to be able to visit you. If we do go back I will have a good try anyhow. I heard from Edith today. They are all well but David's work is very scarce.

How did you get on in your exam? I presume it was the Final Society of Arts that you tried. It is over a year since I failed in that. Doesn't the time fly. Fancy over 12 months since we were at Cosheston. And I have been a "Soldier" (doesn't it sound nice) for nearly eight months.

Have no time to write more now. It is bedtime 10.30. Write and let me know all the news when you have time.

With best love to your Father, Mother, Jack, Wee and Yourself.

I remain,   Yours,   Fred   -//-

Leaving for Front Imminent

May 1915   Written in Pencil

13460

B Coy, 9th Welsh Rgt
Perham Downs
Andover
Hants

Dear Dorothy

Please accept my very best thanks for the photos, letters and P.C. which I received quite safe. You are indeed very kind to have gone to so much trouble for my sake. The photos are indeed very good.

I heard from your mother yesterday. I had just written a P.C. to her when I had the letter. They are having a nice time of it in Wales. You ought to be with them to revisit the place of your birthday (my mistake). But of course, you businesspeople cannot have holidays when you like. Very glad that you have decided to stay in our "job." I think it is better myself anyway until you have more experience.

Your and Jack must be having a good time of it by yourselves. Now is the time for me to visit you.

I am trying for leave this W.E. I don't know if I will succeed, but we are certain to have some before we go. There are a lot of troops leaving here this week so our turn won't be long. But the more troops that go out the quicker will come the "END." And the "END" no one knows, except perhaps John Bull who knows or pretends to know everything. Very busy here now. We are out this week or next for three days and nights in the trenches a few miles away practicing actual warfare. We will of course live there for the time so the sooner it is over the better as I am in no hurry to leave my straw bed!

The Gordon Highlanders who lay next to us here are under orders for the front. No-one is allowed to leave the camp. All their rifles are piled outside the huts ready for them to go at any moment. We will be under the same orders very soon.

That's all now. Excuse black lead. I have done something to my pen and I can get no ink and if I don't write now I don't know when I will be able to again.

With best love to Jack and Yourself

from   Fred-//-

Author's note

Perham Downs *was a military training camp, near Salisbury Plain. Training for the trenches took place there.*

Chin apple hunks

5th May 1915

No. 13460
B. Coy
9th Welsh Rgt
Perham Downs
Andover, Hants

Dear Auntie,   (Dorothy's Mother, Jessie)

Thank you very much for the photos which you were so kind to send. They are really very good and you must have given a lot of your valuable time to do them. Also for the belt. I did not miss it, as I don't usually wear it. I like the one of Jack and myself in the chairs, it is very fine but if I had my feet in front there would be nothing but 'feet' (nearly yards). I would like a few of this photo and a few of myself in the chair. The one with the "smile." I am giving you a lot of trouble and know you have not much time to spare. How did Mollie come out? I would like one of her by herself.

We have been very busy ever since I returned. We have removed into huts and are now very comfortable. We had fresh butter and tinned pears and chunks (chin apple hunks) for tea tonight so you will see that we are doing alright now. We are likely to move from here very soon, probably to Aldershot as there is a scarcity of water here. If we do I will be able to visit you again. They are all well at home. I heard a few days ago. I haven't heard any more about leave but I think we will have it soon There is a big concert here tonight. **George Edward's London Coy** is here so I am just going over. Will write again very soon. Thanking you for your kindness in doing the Photos and for all your kindness to me.

With best love to Uncle, Dorothy, Mollie, Jack & Yourself

I remain your nephew,

Fred -//-

Better Death than Dishonour

30th June 1915

13460
B. Coy,
9th Welsh Rgt.
Perham Downs,
Andover   P.S. Excuse writing paper This is all
I can get until I go to Tidworth

Dear Dorothy (Rusholme, 21 The Drive, Chingford, Essex)

I have been very busy this last week or more or I would have written to you before. Last Wednesday the **King inspected us** here. The whole 19th Division comprising 20,000 men were out. It was a fine sight. Then last Thursday we started firing on the ranges. We were firing all day Sunday and it rained heavy all day. We are out next Thursday and following days a gain.

We have now official orders to the effect that we will leave here on the 17th of next month for active service, so we have not much longer in this country. Don't mention this if you write to Doris as there is no need for them to know as they will only worry. We will be having leave very soon and that will be time enough to tell them.

I heard from home today. Doris is in Pembroke for a holiday. I only wish I was there. I don't think we will be able to arrange a visit here. We don't know what movement may come off any day as we are now under active service conditions. Most of the troops here are out on Sundays trenching, but as yet we have not been out doing that. I am very sorry I would have like for you and Jack to have seen this place but of course it can't be helped.

I am sending a little present to . You will see our badge on it. English for 'Ich Dien' is 'I Serve' and 'Gwell angau na chywilydd' is '**Better Death than Dishonour'** I can't read Welsh myself but I am told that it means this.

We have had very bad weather here lately. Thunder and lightning is very common.

Uncle Tom has gone back to Pontyfrydd. I suppose he has repented.

Nothing else to say this time. Write when you can spare a few minutes of your busy time. Have you decided to stay in your old job? I wish I could have a new job. I am about tired of 'soldiering.' But I will have to finish it now.

Hoping you are all in the best of health.

With best to uncle, Auntie, Jack, and yourself

from Fred-//-

Expecting Germans to Attack Calais

Mid July 1915

13460,
B Coy, 9th Welsh Rgt,
Perham Downs,
Andover.

Dear Auntie

We received orders yesterday that we are to embark next week either Wednesday or Saturday. We don't know what time the orders will come to go. We don't even know where we are going but I think it will be France. All we know is that we are not to be granted leave before we go. We had all been looking forward to having a few days leave and it is a great disappointment for us all. All the troops on the Plains here about **1 ½ million are going out this month** so the Germans, when they make their attack on **Calais,** will have something to put up with. I hope you had a good time in Wales. I sent you a card but I suppose you had left before it got there. Thank you very much for the photos. They were splendid and must have taken you a lot of time to do them. That's all I can say now. **I feel rather miserable because** we are not allowed leave but perhaps it is better so. It would only be saying goodbyes all the time and there is no pleasure in that. I will write again before we sail if I cannot, I will write when we get to somewhere in France."

With best love to you all,

from Fred -/-

Saying Goodbye

17th July 1915

9th Bn Welch Regt. Headed Paper

Dear Dorothy,

This is the last time I will be able to write in this country before we join the Expeditionary Force in France. We leave here tomorrow for some part unknown. I had a very good time at home although it was not very nice saying goodbye. All were quite well at home. Aunt Mary came up to see me. I only had 48 hours so didn't have much to spare. That's all *I can say now.* I will write you as soon as I can after we get out. I have to ask you to do me a kindness. When you write to me will you enclose a sheet of paper and envelope so that I can replay as I cannot carry much out with me. Trusting you are all in the best of health.

With best love to you all from Fred --~-

Now in France

27th July 1915

No 13460 "B" Coy
British Expeditionary Force,
France

Passed by the Censor

Dear Dorothy,

We are having a few days well-earned rest and I have time to write a few letters. I sent Mollie a P.C. I hope she received it. We left England last Sunday week. Sailed from Southampton and landed at Havre the following day. We have been on the move ever since in train – marching and we are now able to hear the big guns firing. We are at present billeted in a little village and are sleeping in barns. We will, I think, be in the trenches early next week.

We have had long marches with our full packs on and we are very glad of the rest. Nothing but soldiers here. All the young men of France are fighting, only the old men, women and children remain. It is a picture that England should copy. I heard from Cosheston yesterday. All Auntie had to say was about a grand wedding down there. They were both quite well. I am getting quite expert at French. It is comical to see us trying to get the people to understand us. Our chaps are delighted with this place as beer is only 10 centimes a glass and it is too weak to make you drunk.

Have nothing to say now. Will write again when I have time. When you can spare a few minutes write to me. It cheers us up to get letters.

Trusting you are all in the best of health.

With best love to Uncle, Auntie, Mollie, Jack & yourself,

I remain

Yours   Fred -//- *Enclose envelope when you write as I am short of them (plenty of paper). F*

Killed by own Artillery

22nd Aug 1915

No 12460
"B" Coy
9th Batt Welsh Rgt
B.E. Force, France

Dear Auntie (Dorothy's mother)

I have plenty of time to write to you today. I sent you a PC yesterday saying I had received your parcel and letter safe. I hope you received this. Let me again thank you for the parcel. You are indeed kind to me. This pad is very handy now. I did not bring one with me as I had no room in my pack and the less weight the better, but now that we are up to the trenches, we have not to carry the pack so far. Some of us are going into the trenches tonight. I don't know if I will go tonight. I have not been warned yet. If not tonight it will be Tuesday. It will only be for 48 hours and when we are relieved, we will go back to base for a time. It is comparatively safe in this part of the line at present. Only the long-distance guns are firing.

We are at present billeted in a village in front of this guns and it is a 'nice' sensation to hear the shells overhead. We were in the second line of trenches which are a quarter of a mile behind the front. Last Friday night we were assisting the R. Es in strengthening the trenches. These trenches were once in the hands of the Huns as all the country around here was. They were at least 60 miles further in France than we are now, last year. They have as well as ourselves been in the trenches they now occupy for months. It will be a big job to get either out of them. We are about 3 kilometres from the front line billeted and the people don't seem frightened at all. A church close here is in ruins. It is an awful sight. Only some of the walls left. While dozens of houses have been absolutely ruined. In the same field as we are camped now are the **1st Batt Seaforth Highlanders**. They are a fine lot. But only 100 of the first lot who came out in September are left.

Most of them were **killed by our own artillery** in a battle which we ought to have won but **owing to someone's mistake we have to fight it again**. This is what the 9th Welsh have to do and there will be no mistake this time. Watch the papers about the 10th of Sept next. There will I think be something happening then.

I can write you this time without the fear of the censor although this letter may be opened at the base. I suppose Dorothy and Jack are having a good time in the Highlands. I hope they will have decent weather. I don't know their address or I would write. But it would take a long time to get there. So the **Zeps** have been worrying you again. They made another miscalculation though. But it is a pity for the civil population. There are plenty of planes up here today and both sides are trying to shell them. It is a fine sight. There is a very heavy bombardment too. Sunday is a favourite day with both sides. There is an Indian Division attached to ours and they are a fine lot of chaps especially the **Gurkhas.** Enormous lot of them here.

Well, that is enough about the war. I can't always write to you like this. We are only allowed one envelope like this a week and I give it turns to you. I heard from Dad yesterday. They are all well. The girls are still in Pembrokeshire and having a good time. I have not heard from Edith for some time. Very glad that you liked the P.C. The French are skilled in this sort of work. It is very good of Alice to offer her services but I do think she had better stay where she is. She is in a good place now I think and is of course doing her 'bit' here. Remember me to her when you write. I don't know her address. Well I think you will have enough to do to find time to read all this. **I will give the Huns something back on Walthamstow's account tonight if I have the chance.** Trusting you are quite well. Will write again when we come out.

Best love to you all

from Fred

xxxxx .

In The Trenches

9th Sept 1915 **Thursday**

13460
B Coy 9th
Welsh Rgt,
BE Force, France   This letter was not censored

My dear Dorothy,

I have now time to write to you in answer to your letter. I must apologize for not doing so before but I really have had no time. I will now start my epistle.

Last Sunday week we left the base on our way to the firing line. We halted that night about 6 miles from the line. We started on Monday morning and halted at Mid-day in a woods to wait for the "darkness of the night." It was here that I wrote to the P.C. after writing we heard from the General's staff that the Dardanelles were forced, and that accounts for my P.S. on the card. Of course that has turned out to be false and our excitement was all for nothing. That night we reached the reserve trenches and stayed there until Saturday night. From here we used to go in the night on fatigue work to the R. E's and trench digging under fire.

I think it was on Thursday night that the Germans found out that we were out and started the Machine Guns on us. They kept this up for a half-hour and then stopped thinking they had wiped us out but we had plenty of sandbags for cover and no one got hit. They also shelled our dug outs in the attempt to get the range of our guns which were all around us.

Then on Saturday night last we moved on to the firing line. We had over 2 miles of trenches to go through and we were up to our knees in some places in mud. It had rained for a few days and this accounted for the mud. We have been in the firing line since then and I don't know exactly how long we will stay here. We have only had a few casualties, 1 killed and four wounded. The lines are about four hundred yards apart and we are on the most advanced part of the British Line. They are preparing for an advance on our left to bring their line up to ours. This is held by the Queen's Kent Regt. "The Buffs"

In front of us the Germans hold a hill and if we could only get the possession of this we would soon be fighting in German territory. I am told from the top of this hill you can see the Valley of the Rhine and it is on the slope all the way. We are preparing for this and if we get them over the hill I think they will 'chuck up the sponge.'

Our field trench artillery are pelting them all day and they don't retaliate much. I don't know if they are short of ammunition.

Well that's enough of war. It is only every now and again that we get one of these envelopes which are not censored that is why I am able to write like this. Very sorry to hear that Auntie is not well. Do hope by this time that she is better. I sent you a P.C a few days ago. It was the official card. I hope you had it alright. The picture P.Cs (*postcards*)that I send were bought back in the base, there are of course no shops here. There are civilians nearer than five miles and we can do without them.

They are of the sort that you only like when they are at a distance. They would rob you of your shoelaces. There are more "pubs" in France now than there has ever been but the beer is harmless, no alcohol whatever in it. The wine is very good but rather expensive. The best drink here is coffee and you can't get better than French coffee. It is fine and you get a nice basin full (no cups in France) for 10 centimes. The bread which they bake is also very good but of course we get the army bread. We buy the French bread as a luxury whenever we can get it. I would give a 5 franc note for one now anyhow.

Thanks for the offer of some magazines. They would be very acceptable out here. We get the London papers every day but of course they are a few days behind date but we can't get any magazines. Thanks also for the offer of the "illigant" (*sic*) socks. I don't know what sort they are. I am not in want of them at the present. We have all, at present, enough to go on with and we can't carry any more. You will understand this when I tell you that our base is about ten miles back and we have to march this * with full pack, rifle and 300 rounds of ammunition. So we don't like carrying anything more than is absolutely necessary. Later they will be very acceptable.

This is of course when we go back for a rest

Tell Mollie I will be very pleased to get a photo of herself and I will keep it in my wallet. I have her pad still and mean to try and keep it.

You have by now settled down to work again I suppose. I hope the change did you both good.

The weather is lovely here now. The trenches have dried up fine and I am just getting clean after Saturday night. We were in an awful state and I had, just before leaving, received a parcel from Edith. I had to carry this as well as my full kit. I was glad that I did carry it as we were short of rations for a day or two. All well at home. I heard from Dad a few days ago. They have all finished their holidays. Also heard from Cosheston. They are both well there. Nothing to talk about down there only about the new aero plane sheds they are building or going to build at Carew.

Well that's all now I think this will make up for lost time. I think I have told you everything but where we are and you must have to guess at that.

Hoping you are all in the best of health. With best love to you all

I remain

Yours   Fred ---

Fred's Last Letter to Dorothy

11th September 1915

13460 "B" Coy, 9th Welsh Rgt, BEF France

Sunday

Dear Dorothy

Thanks very much for your two letters. I have not had time this last week. Very glad that you are enjoying (or is it that you enjoyed them) your holidays. I suppose you are now back home and I expect you like starting work again and now I never did. But in the army your likes are never considered and you generally find it is what you dislike that you have to do. I wrote a PC to yesterday and said that I was going to the trenches again. Our Batt were in them last week and we had a short rest after. This morning we started off again. We heard on the march that the Dardanelles had been forced and must say it cheered us up considerably. Now we won't be long and I am now hoping to be home for my Xmas dinner this year. But we have something to do first.

Monday

Had no time to finish this letter yesterday. I am writing this while we are halting on the march. We are waiting for dusk to get into the trenches. The Germans are generally on the lookout for the new men going into the trenches. It is the most dangerous part of the business –the going in.

Have not much to say this time. Thank you for correcting my French. I must have got mixed up and my French is very elementary.

I will write again as soon as I can. Write when you have time. Always pleased to hear from you but don't be too hard on me if I keep you waiting a little.

Trusting that your holidays did you both good.

with best love to you all,

from Fred -//-

Figure 17 Cardiff Castle Memorial

Fred's name among them.

Figure 18 Fred with cousin, Jack

Welsh Regiment 9th Btn

9th (Service) Battalion, Welsh Regiment was raised at Cardiff on the 9th of September 1914 as part of Kitchener's Second New Army and joined 58th Brigade, 19th (Western) Division. They trained on Salisbury Plain and moved into billets in Basingstoke in November 1914 for the winter. In January they moved to Weston Super Mare and to Perham Downs in May 1915 for final training. They proceeded to France, landing at Boulogne in mid July 1915, the division concentrating near St Omer. Their first action was at Pietre, in a diversionary action supporting the Battle of Loos.

- See more at:
http://www.wartimememoriesproject.com/greatwar/allied/alliedarmy-view.php?pid=1035#sthash.vcbxlAM1.dpuf

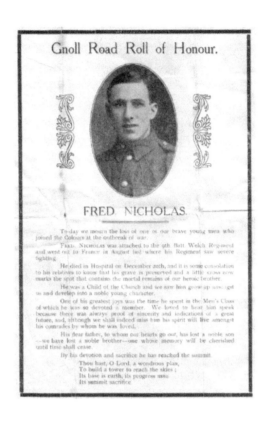

Gnoll Road Roll of Honour.

FRED NICHOLAS.

To-day we mourn the loss of one of our brave young men who joined the Colours at the outbreak of war.

FRED. NICHOLAS was attached to the 9th Batt. Welch Regiment and went out to France in August last where his Regiment saw severe fighting.

He died in Hospital on December 20th, and it is some consolation to his relatives to know that his grave is preserved and a little cross now marks the spot that contains the mortal remains of our heroic brother.

He was a Child of the Church and we saw him grow up amongst us and develop into a noble young character.

One of his greatest joys was the time he spent in the Men's Class of which he was so devoted a member. We loved to hear him speak because there was always proof of sincerity and indication of a great future, and, although we shall indeed miss him his spirit will live amongst his comrades by whom he was loved.

His dear father, to whom our hearts go out, has lost a noble son —we have lost a noble brother—one whose memory will be cherished until time shall cease.

By his devotion and sacrifice he has reached the summit.

Thou hast, O Lord, a wondrous plan,
To build a tower to reach the skies ;
Its base is earth, its progress man
Its summit sacrifice

Figure 19 Gnoll Roll of Honour

Fred's letters to his friend Ben

Fred wrote several letters to his good friend Ben which are held in the archives in his hometown in Neath, Glamorgan, Wales where there is a memorial. Copies of the letters were sent to me by Anne Lee and I have decided to include them. They give an insight into the thoughts of a young man facing the prospect of going to war and the stoicism he and his friends showed through the most horrific of battles, experiencing many weeks under heavy fire in the trenches, thinking of home and the times they shared before the war and their hopes of returning 'safe and in good health.'

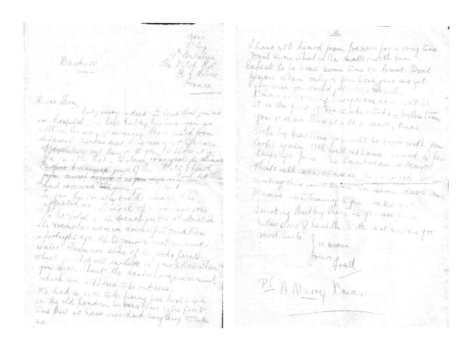

Figure 20 One of Fred's Letters to Ben

49 Reading Rd
Basingstoke

18 December 1914

Dear Ben,

You will see by the above address that I am at last back in civilization again, but I am sorry to say that it is not for long. We came here last Monday and we leave here tomorrow (Saturday) for Perham Downs (S. Plain) near Ludgershall. We have to start our firing course there on the butts on Sunday. This means of course that there will not be any leave at Xmas. Its d...rotten. I had been looking forward to being home then. We shall be there about 10 days and as soon as we finish we will be able to have a furlough. I am now hoping to be home on New Year's day. Fancy spending Xmas day on Salisbury Plain. Think of me when you are eating your Xmas dinner at home as I hope you will be able to. It would not be so bad if they left us here, where we are so comfortable, but to have the cheek to send us back to the plain is awful. I am writing Joe to let him know. I heard from him a short time ago. I don't feel like writing anymore now. I feel like Barney's Bull. Remember me to all at home when you see them. Hoping that you will be able to have leave and that you will enjoy your Xmas

      is the wish of

        your friend Fred

1 Manilla Crescent,
Birnbeck Road
Weston-Super-Mare

22 December 1914

Dear Ben,

How are you getting on after this long time? We are still in the same place. We had orders last Sunday week to leave for Tidworth Barracks on the following Wednesday but they were cancelled. We went to Cheddar for three days last week. We slept in a Tea Room on a Concrete floor, so we were not sorry to return to our feather bed. It was in orders last night that the Batt will leave here the end of this month for Perham Downs so we are making the most of the time. When do you go? We may yet go together. We had our new equipment this week. It is leather not webbing like the old. The officers are to have the same. It looks all right but it take a deuce of a time to put it together. There are nearly 100 buckles.

I heard from Joe last week for the first time since Xmas. He said that you had given him my address. He is hoping to get to London very soon. If it wasn't for this war, I might have been there by the way I was 21 last Monday (15th). Aren't we getting old? I will have the Old age pension when…………………..

Note: The rest of this letter is missing

23 December 1914

Dear Ben,

I have just rec'd your letter dated 17th inst. You must have received my letter after you sent this one.

Very glad that you have succeeded in getting leave over Xmas. You must count yourself very lucky. I hope to be home next Wednesday. We have finished the first half of our firing and hope to finish next Sunday. It is a fine experience firing and I am glad to say that I have done very well so far.

We hope to be back in Basingstoke next Monday. There is 'Khaki' there for us. We hope to be able to start leaving Wednesday. I am so sorry I won't be able to see you. We never know where we shall meet again, perhaps on a battlefield on the Continent.

Hoping that you will spend a very happy Xmas along with your parents and sisters.

Remember me to them, also to Jonah and the members of the class. We will be firing on Xmas day. Think of me when you are having a happy time. Remember me to Joe and his girl if you see her.

That's all now.

With best wishes from

Your sincere friend,

Fred//

No 13460

"B" Coy
9th Batt
Welsh Regt.
Perham Downs
Andover, Hants

19 May 1915

Dear Ben,

Thanks very much for your letter. I had been expecting to hear from you for some time and I was beginning to think that you had gone out. But very glad that you are still in this country and that you are quite well. I don't think we will be long after you as we are to have our Rifles this week and we will then be fully equipped. The whole of our Division (the 19th)are close here now, A.S.C, RE. FRA RAMC and everything so we won't be here much longer. The R.E.s and the A.S.C. are on your old camp at Tidworth Park and there is a brigade of Highlanders at Parkhouse. I was there a few days ago and it looked a lot better than it did when we left it. We were supposed to go out for 3 days roughing this morning, but it was cancelled so we had a Brigade day instead out at 8 back at 7 so I am fagged. Very glad that you had a decent time at home. I hope to be home soon although I am not very anxious as I don't like saying Goodbye. We don't know where we will meet next, perhaps in France, but I hope at home and before very long. I am about sick of it. If you have time to write before you go, do, if not write as soon after as you can. Nothing to say this time. Hoping that this will find you in the best of health as it leaves

your old friend

Fred//

"B" Coy
9th Battl
Welsh Regt.
Perham Downs
Andover, Hants

June 1915

Dear Ben,

I heard three weeks ago that 12th had gone out, but today some of our boys said they had seen some of the 8th Welsh so I am writing, hoping that you are not gone out. Although I suppose you are, like me, sick of it and a change would be very acceptable. We are now in huts and we are very comfortable although Weston was better.

Very busy this week. King and Kitchener are coming on Wednesday to inspect us. We are now fully equipped and I don't expect we will be here much longer.

Have not been home since Easter. I was in London a fortnight ago and had a very good time and expect to be home on final leave very soon. We are doing final firing now and then will be fully trained. Four bulls and 1 chipper on the 200 yards today. Not bad is it?

Have not heard from Joe for some time. I must write him when I have time. I heard from Jonah some time ago. Teddy Morgans was in Gnoll Road yesterday. I tried to get leave but could only get until Sunday night owing to the firing.

Now write and let me know all the news as soon as you can. No news here.

Muriel wishes to be remembered to you. I still write to her.

With best wishes as to your health and also success when you go out.

from Your old friend Fred//

The following letters were all written from The Front so were censored.

13460 'B' Coy,
 British Expeditionary Force,
France

28 July 1915

Dear Ben,

I was delighted to receive you letter a few days ago. I had made several enquiries at home about you, but had not heard anything. You will see by the above address that we are also on active service. We left Southampton on July 18th and landed at Havre the following day. We had a train ride from there and have been on the march since. We are now having a few days rest before we get to the trenches. We can hear the sound of the big guns firing so we will soon be in the thick of it. There are a tremendous lot of Huns troops out here now. There will be a big move forward soon then we will have both been under fire.   Let us hope that we will both get through quite safe and that many happy times are still in store for us both.

I haven't heard from Jonah yet. Your parents and sisters were quite well when I saw them a week before we came out. All were well at home and were all asking if I had any news of you. I will not say anything about your going on to the Dardanelles. Your mother said you were going or at least she thinks so.

Wyndham Williams was out here some time. Billy Cooks and Ken Collins and that lot are a few miles behind us. You ought to be here with me but perhaps you are better where you are. Did not see Joe when he was home. Only had 48 hrs so I had not time to spare. MJR and Miss T all wish to be remembered to you.

That's all now. With best wishes for a speedy and safe return

     I remain Your Sincere Friend   Fred//

22 August 1915

Sunday

Dear Ben,

I wrote to you a month ago on receiving your letter but have not yet heard from you. But I suppose it takes a good time to reach you. We have now been in this country five weeks and I have not yet fallen in love with it. I saw the Western Mail a few days ago and read that the 8th RWE were in action so I suppose you have been under fire by this time. We are going into the trenches tonight for 48 hours. You can't stand much more than that at a time. Lively here today. Always is on a Sunday. It is a favourite day with both artilleries. I have not heard from Joe for some time. I will write to him again. What do you think of the war? Is there any sign of it finishing out with you? There is no sign of weakness with the enemy here. I wish it would finish if it was only to get back to Maths (sic) again. Fancy 12 months today we went home for Cardiff. It seems like 12 years.

MJR wishes to be remembered to you. She said she was going to write to you. I don't know if she has. "Sunday" in France. Doesn't it sound nice. Waiting for the pub to open to have a glass of Wine. All well at home. I heard yesterday. That's all now. Write when you have time. trusting that you are quite safe and well. With best wishes

from

your friend   Fred/

4 October 1915

Monday

Dear Ben,

I was delighted to receive your letter of the 14th and to hear that you are quite safe and well. Things are rather quiet here now after the hard time we had last weekend, the result of which you have heard by this time I am sure. We were in the middle of it as usual with The Welsh came out with honours. On Saturday the 25th we made a charge on the German trenches, as did our whole line. We attained our object but not without loss. My pal Jack Williams the Barber. I don't know if you know him was killed also Jack Lloyd. You know Jack Lloyd. He was in our tent at Parkhouse. All the rest of our boys except one or two who were wounded came out safe. We and the R. Welsh Fus. made the attack for this Brigade and the Cheshires and Wilts were the support. Can't tell you much about it because of the censor, but it is my opinion that this is the beginning of the end. We are still keeping up the attack and further successes are anticipated.

Very glad to see that you have such ?? opinions about France. But speaking for myself I have nothing of what you speak. We have been in the trenches for five weeks on a stretch and I have only had one drink in that time. The only place we can get anything is miles away from here, but I am hoping to have a bust up when we get back for a rest which ought to be very soon. My nerves want a rest after being under this awful bombardment.

Heard from Joe a short time ago. He was quite well and said he was writing to you. I think he will soon be knocking it off but I asked him to wait until we returned. If he did not he would lose our presence. I wrote a few lines to your Mother last week. Have you heard from Jonah Arnold yet?

All well at home. Heard today. Nothing more to say now. Hoping that you will be spared to return and then we will make up for lost time. Trusting that you are in the best of health as it leaves

Your sincere friend, Fred//

27 October 1915

Wednesday

Dear Ben,

Very pleased to receive yours of the 4th inst. You have no doubt by this time received my last letter. It takes such a long time (about a fortnight I believe) for a letter to reach you. Why didn't you come over here with us? We can get letters from home here in two days.

I was indeed glad to get your letter as there were nasty rumours at home regarding Oscar Williams and yourself, but I am indeed glad to hear that you are quite safe. I don't know if it is true that Oscar is in hospital in England. I heard from home to this effect. I hope anyhow that it is not serious. Tell me about it in your next. I met him when I was home last Xmas. I think it was. Fancy it twelve months since we were on the Plains, we are getting old sweats are we not?

I told you in my last about our part in the big advance. We lost heavily. Most of our officers are gone. You know young Lieut. Owens, he was I think about the first to join us. He was wounded in the charge and has died since in hospital. I don't think you know any of the rest. We have a very decent lot again now, equal, if not better than the old ones.

We have been out for a fortnight's rest since our last action and came in last Sunday. But it is only a short visit this time I think, about 10 days (the last time we were in for 40)

Some of ours have been on leave and all of us will get 7 days sometime next month. So of course I am looking forward to it. We have been here well over three months now. Only wish it were possible for you to have the same.

All well at home. Muriel Roberts has sent you a PC. I hope you will receive it all right. She said she thought it would cheer you up a little. She is not so bad after all.

It was in the Church magazine that I had written a very interesting letter from the trenches. I suppose this is Mady Ree's work.

Well Ben, that's all this time. I hope it will (as your officers think) be soon over with you out there. I thought, myself, that the Germans were too safely entrenched here but it is wonderful what British troops can shift.

Let's hope that it will soon be over and that we may resume our ordinary toils and forget all that we have seen.

You will no doubt be glad to hear that Will Thomas is acting company quartermaster sergeant. Will Lavarack is in hospital, something the matter with his eyes. EH was asking about you when I last saw him and wishes to be remembered to you all. Hoping to hear from you again when you have time. With best wishes as to health and safety,

I remain, your sincere chum, Fred/

PS/ Tom Mahoney one of boys wishes to know if Jerry Healy is safe. He thinks he is with you and wishes to be remembered to you. F//

13460
B Coy , 9th Battalion
The Welsh Regiment
R.E. Force, France

1 December 1915

Dear Ben,

Very sorry indeed to hear that you are in hospital but hope that by this time you are well on the way to recovery. I have heard from different sources that there are a lot of cases of dysentery out there with you. I suppose it is the country that is to blame or any rate the climate. Before I received yours of the 18th I heard from Muriel Robert that you were in hospital. She had received a letter from you she said. So far this country nor the climate has affected me. Several of ours have gone to hospital with trench feet and rheumatism. The trenches were in an awful condition a fortnight ago. Up to your waist in mud and water. These are some of the good points which you did not include in your letters when you wrote about the canteens and amusements which are supposed to be out here. We had a ride to the firing line last week in the old London buses. This is the first-time that we have ever had anything to take us.

I have not heard from Joe now for a long time. Don't know what is the matter with him. Expect to be home sometime on leave. Don't know when, only a few have gone as yet. Only wish you could get it as well. Xmas is coming very close now isn't it. It is the first of December today, by the time you get this it will be nearly Xmas. Hope that by that time you will be with your Corps again. All well at home. Heard a few days ago. Jones the Cambrian is Mayor.

That's all now. Excuse the scribble. I am writing this in a barn in semi-darkness. We are having a few weeks rest.

Trusting that by this time you are in a better state of health. With best wishes for good luck

I remain Yours. Fred //   PS/ Merry Xmas

Fred died just 19 days after this letter was written and 4 days after his 22nd birthday.

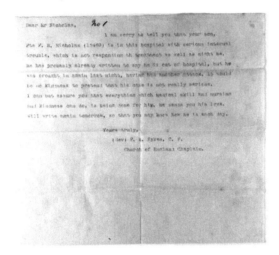

Figure 21 B.E.F. Message -Fred Gravely Ill

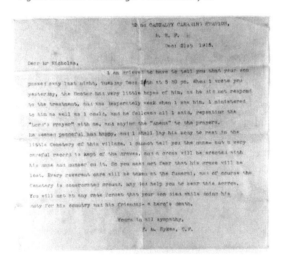

Figure 22 B.E.F. Message - Fred Has Died

21 December 1915 A hero's death.

These letters were received by Fred's father, Hugh Nicholas, who was Dorothy's uncle. He received his son's War Gratuity of £5 in August 1919.

DOROTHY MARGARET NICHOLAS

BIOGRAPHY

Dorothy was born 13 APR 1896 • Cardiff, Glamorgan, Wales to David Nicholas and Jessie Bignal Brock. Her brother John (Jack) was born two years later. In 1901 at the age of 4, Dorothy moved with her parents to Brooklyn, New York, USA where her father, a ship's architect was employed by Lloyds Shipping Company inspecting ships. The family returned to England in 1911 and lived at 21 The Drive, Chingford, Essex. Dorothy's sister Mollie, who was born in Brooklyn, was 1 year old. In 1915, Dorothy, at the age of 19, qualified as a shorthand-typist and bookkeeper.

During 1916, Dorothy and her mother, Jessie, started accepting letters from servicemen, including Frederick Hugh Nicholas, a cousin and Tony More who later became related through marriage. Many of the letters were sent either from the 'Front' or from a military rehabilitation hospital. Some were sent prior to the war from various training camps. Dorothy qualified as a Red Cross Nurse and worked at Brookfield Hospital, *Hale End for the rest of WW1. Most of the letters are addressed to Dorothy at her home in Chingford. Many of the envelopes are marked with a stamp 'Passed by the Censor' and she often marked the envelope with the date as having been 'answered.'

In January 1923, Dorothy married farmer William James Fordham Soper at Epping, Essex and they lived at Nightingale Farm, Edmonton, London where they had three children, Elizabeth Jean, David Malcom and Andrew James. David died at the age of 1. They moved to farm at Harlow, Essex before the second world war and Dorothy used her secretarial skills to keep the books for the family business. She died in August 1946 from cancer of the colon, just a month before the author, Diana Helen, her first grandchild, was born.

Figure 23 Dorothy's Red Cross War Medal

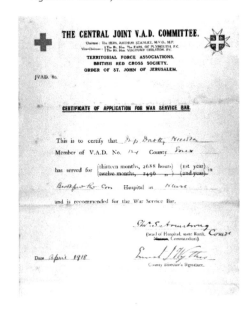

Figure 24 Dorothy's Application for War Service

Figure 25 Graduation Exercises Brooklyn N.Y.

Figure 26 Dorothy's Qualification Certificate 1915

In July 1915, Dorothy was working for a publishing firm in Fleet Street, London. She wrote a letter to her friend Connie, a relative of 'IRVINE,' in Brooklyn, N.Y. It tells of her intention to train to be a Red Cross Nurse and also her observations about the young men injured in the war. It seems that the letter was never sent as it was among her letters from the men at the front.

Fleet Street
London, E.C.
27th July 1915

Dear Connie,

I expect that you will jump to the conclusion that I am in business when you see the heading. I started here in May, and so far I like it very well. I am with a publishing firm and the work is very interesting. Just now the other girl is off on her three week's holiday, so I get a bit more work to do, though not much, as this is the slack time. I have been waiting to write to you until I saw how things were going between germany (sic) (no capitals allowed for that place) and U.S. Seemingly there is just to be an interchange of polite notes and excuses between them, so I had better not put off any longer. Honestly I cannot understand the U.S. a bit. It seems to us over here that she is letting herself get sat upon very easily. Yesterday when I saw that another American ship had been sunk I thought that would bring things to a head, but from this morning's papers nothing seems to be going to happen. However I like the States too well to think that they are not acting for the best, even if it does seem a bit slow to me. The great question we ask when an American ship is sunk is "What do you think the Americans will do this time?" and the same answer usually is "Why write and ask germany please not to do it again." But to tell the truth, I hope that the U.S. won't feel that it must join in. The War is really terrible enough as it is, and the more men that come into it only makes the loss greater. I don't think the germans will ever win, but they certainly are putting up a stiff fight, even if it is not in the least bit honourable. I am afraid that we are getting very bitter over here, but can you blame us? Really, Connie, if you could see some of the fine young fellows that have been back from France perfectly ruined, either through wounds, or worse still when they have been 'gassed' it would make your blood boil, just as it does ours. It is so pitiful to see a great big man being led around, because the gas fumes have ruined his eyes.

This letter will be more like a lecture by the time I finish it, but just now I can't help it. I am going to start this week to learn Red Cross Work. It will be some time before I can do anything, but I am just 19, and as a rule they will not let you do any nursing till you are 21, but I would pass for 30 any day, (or at least they tell me so at home)

I have not sent you any newspapers yet. Nor have I received any from you. I suppose that they are held back for some reason, but I don't see what harm they could do. Still we must do as we are told just now and ask very few questions. I really have no interesting news to tell you. Life is about as dull as it can be. It is rather a pity that we who are just about 20 should not have any of the usual fun, that you are supposed to enjoy then. There is absolutely nothing to do just now. At night everyone sits at home. Of course there are tennis courts just the same, and theatres and other things, but you feel so mean when you are playing tennis and think of all the boys who were playing you last year and now are "Somewhere" either in France or the Dardanelles. Several of the Chingford fellows are in Egypt and at the Dardanelles, while one at least is in India. We had a letter from him the other day and he says he is very homesick and tired of black faces and heat. He has just recovered from rheumatic fever, so perhaps he isn't quite up to the mark yet. My Welsh cousin, Fred Nicholas, went away from England last Sunday week, but we have never heard yet where he has gone to or whether he has arrived yet. There is usually a delay in getting letters from the front, and we all dread reading casualty lists. All the boys have numbers, and they calmly tell us that if anything happens to them we had better look out for their numbers in the lists. You ought to be glad that you are out of the whole thing. How would you like to have feelings in you.

I saw a german (sic) woman on Sunday who was married to an Englishman (or at any rate he is supposed to be English, though his name sounds bit fishy). Of course she is safe and happy in England, and doesn't mind the War a bit. She told one shopkeeper that everything depended upon what her 'dear kaiser said." Well, when I got up behind her on Sunday, there was nothing I would have enjoyed more than jamming my umbrella right through her and then opening it. I suppose this will shock your feelings, but never mind, I am a long way off and I don't trouble you very often with my views, do I? I must stop typing now, but I will finish this sometime today. Mollie is having a concert at her school this afternoon and she is going to be in a song. I wish I could go and see   her sing, but business is too grasping.

Author's note: The 'g' in lower case for German is deliberate.

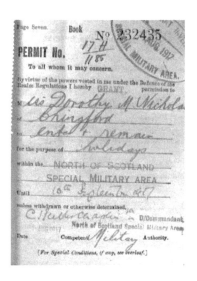

Figure 27 Permit for travel to Scotland

Permit was issued by the Metropolitan Police for Dorothy to stay in North of Scotland Special
Military Area in September 1917 for a holiday. Dorothy had a number of relatives in Scotland.

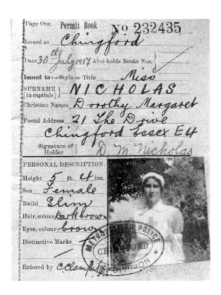

Figure 28 Identity Document

Figure 29 Dorothy's Permit Book

Figure 30 Dorothy with her father David Nicholas (1857-1935)

Ship's Surveyor for Lloyds Registry of Shipping

David became a Shipwrights' Apprentice to the Royal Navy in March 1877
at the age of 14 and later became a Master of the Merchants' Service in 1891.
He also found himself in Japan giving the Japanese advice on building steel ships.
The family moved back to Chingford, Essex from the USA just prior to WW1.

A Sense of Humour

Letter written on headed paper

Whipps Cross War Hospital
Whipps Cross Road
Leytonstone,
London E11
Registered under the War Charities Act 1916

6.3.19

Dear Daddy,

The terrible strain of excessive letter writing is now beginning to tell on me. Mother is also suffering, as you already know. We go about with anxiously searching eyes, searching for something to write about. My, won't we have a high tea when you return. I half think you are adopting the 'Daily Mirror' idea that it is best for husbands and wives to spend only weekends together, as otherwise they become 'fed up' with each other's society. Better watch out that Mother, Mollie and I don't follow the same creed, and depart, as Mollie used to suggest, for our holidays, she to Wales, me to Scotland, and best of all, Mother to Clapton, all to reunite at stated intervals. How is that for a sound scheme to prolong the family unity as per 'Daily Mirror'?

You will by this time, no doubt, have been struck with this paper. A very ancient old man came up to the ward kitchen yesterday and handed me a bundle of paper and envelopes 'for the soljers' (*sic*). So being a bit of a soljer (*sic*) myself, I took these two sheets as a war memento. Perhaps you will be good enough to return these sheets some time, so that we can have something to show for my 2 ½ years of army life.

I am sorry I forget to tell you we were very pleased with my costume. The only fault is that the skirt is a bit too short, so I am going into town this afternoon to ask Mr. Palmer to lengthen it a little. That will be quite easily done. The coat is a fine fit and makes me look about forty. (Mother says that is not true, but it really gives me a fine 'figure')

This paper may be all very lovely, but it is the very dickens to write on. The pen grows a plentiful beard in three lines.

This is such a nice bright day that I am sorry to be going into town, however, can't be helped. Probably new neighbours will be in by the tie you return, but you have a fine excuse all readymade for neglecting our garden this year, as Mrs. Maloney has sent over for the roller. Without implements, of course and obviously, it is impossible to do any work.

You need not bother about your cobbling suit as Mother is making you a new one from that green and red plaid shawl we have had in the house for such a time. She hopes you won't mind the fringe round the foot. Of course you won't often be outside in it, so it won't matter much.

Mother has brought in the dinner. Yorkshire pudding (and they say leather is short, I wonder why). Never mind, good teeth are more than coronets.

> Hoping to see you soon
> > With love
> > > Dorothy

Short story by Dorothy written on Thursday Night at 10 o'clock on the 9th September 1915

Waiting for an Air-raid

We are passing through an experience which we may never see again (& I hope not). For two successive nights there have been zeppelin raids and pretty bad ones too, and tonight from various different sources we have had word that 5 to 8 infernal machines are on their way here. This waiting is almost worse than the actual occurrence. Word has been sent round to put out all lights and consequently candles are being used as faint illuminations. Somehow life is very different just now. One hardly knows what to say or do. My mouth is horribly dry and uncomfortable. We are spending the time going from the dining-room through to the road to ask if anything has been heard yet and then coming back. At least mother and I are doing that while Daddy and Jack are standing at the gate. I am just on edge, waiting to hear one bang. We have Mollie down with us tonight as we feel safer when she is near. I carried her out of bed and she never attempted to wake. Jack didn't get home till 9 o'clock tonight and he brought the news that word had been received at the Docks that 5 or more zeppelins were on the way. Cheerful sort of evening news. I wish if they were coming they would come and get it over with. I will write no more just now but just wait and see. I wish I could tell what I may write to finish this. But even so near a future is unknowable.

> They didn't come after all
> > Stung again.

Acknowledgements

First of all I would like to say how thankful I am to be able to acknowledge my grandmother, Dorothy Margaret Nicholas, whom I sadly never met. It has been a great pleasure as well as a fascination for me to read the many letters and see the many photographs she left the family among her belongings.

I wish to acknowledge the several resources from where I found information about the young men who wrote the many letters to my grandmother: Wikipedia, for in relevant information about Hale End Hospital and Brookfield, The British Journal of Nursing April 20, 1918, p 277 - Information about Bangour Hospital, Military-Genealogy.com, Wartime Memories Project-http://www.wartimememoriesproject.com, Ancestry.co.uk- my family tree research, www.greatwarforum.org – for further information about Private George Leonard Sweetnam.

I also wish to thank Anne Lee, great niece of Frederick Hugh Nicolas for copies of Fred's letter to Ben, his friend from Wales and also for the photos of the war memorial in Cardiff Castle and the *Gnoll Roll of Honour.*

I am pleased also to acknowledge Raymond Sweetman for providing further information about George Leonard Sweetnam, a distant cousin of his whose name has a different spelling and who contacted me when he discovered I had made connections on the Sweetnam/Sweetman family tree.

My brother, William Filip Moen, for sending me a number of documents in his possession from the family paraphernalia, in particular the two letters that Frederick's father, Hugh, received regarding his son's death in France at the age of twenty-two.

My good friend Eileen Gaudion who found my typos and gave me some very useful advice.

My husband John Pritchard for his encouragement to complete the book and his patience while I transcribed the letters and got the book together finally after, not days, not weeks, not months but quite a number of years.

INDEX

GLOSSERY

The Board – Referred to in many of the letters. The Medical Evaluation Board (MEB) is a process designed to determine whether a Service member's long-term medical condition enables him to continue to meet medical the standards needed to be retained for service.

Perham Downs was a military training camp, near Salisbury Plain. Training for the trenches took place there.

General Sir Horace Lockwood Smith-Dorrien, GCB GCMG DSO ADC (26 May 1858 – 12 August 1930) was a British soldier. In the spring of 1915 he commanded British Second Army at the Second Battle of Ypres. He was relieved of command by French for requesting permission to retreat from the Ypres Salient to a more defensible position.

Dr. Louisa Garrett Anderson, CBE (28 July 1873 – 15 November 1943) was a medical pioneer, a member of the Women's Social and Political Union, a suffragette, and social reformer.

Chingford, Essex – Where Dorothy lived with her parents during WW1.

Sobraon Barracks, Colchester – Was a military heart hospital.

War Loan - A *war* bond is an initiative by a government to fund *military* operations and spending by issuing *debt* for the public to *purchase*.

Photographs

Diana Helen Pritchard, brought up in Western Canada, the daughter of immigrants from England and Norway, has written her autobiography 'My Paths to Freedom' and produced several books of poetry, including 'One Wrong Foot' influenced by her Canadian childhood. She now lives in Guernsey, Channel Islands

Diana has deciphered and translated a number of letters written to her English grandmother, Dorothy Margaret Nicholas, a Red Cross nurse, by servicemen she corresponded with during WW1. These letters were written either directly from *The Front* or from various convalescent hospitals and several were stamped *Passed by the Censor*.

Included are photos and notes about the servicemen as well as a brief look at the life of Dorothy.

Printed in Great Britain
by Amazon

20144082R10081